History

AGES 9-11

Kath Cox
Gillian Goddard
Pat Hughes

CONTENTS

Authors
Kath Cox
Gillian Goddard
Pat Hughes

Editor
Christine Lee

Assistant Editor
Dulcie Booth

Series designer
Lynne Joesbury

Designer
Sarah Rock

Illustrations
David Wyatt

Cover photograph
Digital Vision Ltd

Published by
Scholastic Ltd,
Villiers House,
Clarendon Avenue,
Leamington Spa,
Warwickshire
CV32 5PR
Text © 2000 Kath Cox, Gillian Goddard and Pat Hughes
© 2000
Scholastic Ltd
1 2 3 4 5 6 7 8 9 0
0 1 2 3 4 5 6 7 8 9

British Library Cataloguing-in-Publication Data
A catalogue record for this book is available from the British Library.

ISBN 0-439-01810-2

The right of Kath Cox, Gillian Goddard and Pat Hughes to be identified as the Authors of this work has been asserted by her in accordance with the Copyright, Designs and Patents Act 1988.

Introduction

This book is aimed at teachers who are responsible for planning, teaching, assessing and reporting the curriculum for nine- to eleven-year-olds. Curriculum 2000 gives teachers a fairly broad brief for when they teach different history units, while the QCA scheme of work suggests that some units may be more appropriate in specific years. In this book we are following the QCA recommendations that children in Years 5 and 6 cover Ancient Greece, the Victorians and Britain since 1930. We have chosen to look at the Aztecs, rather than the Indus Valley civilisation, as our experience in visiting primary schools suggests that this unit is the more popular one for a non-European study. The Ancient Greeks, the Victorians and Britain since 1930 contain a strong element of local history.

Some schools may have planned to teach some of these units earlier in the Key Stage, in which case the lesson plans will need adapting for a younger age group. Other schools may not be covering all four units or may decide to spend more time on one unit and less on another. The plans are simply a suggested structure and should be changed and adapted as necessary to support the long-term history planning in the school, the specific needs and interests of the children in the class or year group and the historical dimension of the local environment.

There are four themed chapters in this book, each covering one history unit. Each chapter is divided into two units of work. The units are often complementary to each other and therefore you should choose one or other as appropriate to your needs. Most of the units form the basis of a substantial chunk of history work – perhaps over half a term – and by providing progressive lesson plans show how history can be sequenced. The grids at the beginning of each unit are intended to aid medium-term planning, and highlight the enquiry questions covered by the lesson plans. The grids can also be used to help plan links that history has with other subjects across the curriculum, especially literacy, numeracy and art. ICT links are given within the lesson plans themselves.

The introductions to each chapter and unit provide some background information that you may find useful when working with the lesson plans, and further information is given in the lesson plans themselves.

Why is history important?

Before a subject can be taught well the teacher must understand what is most important and why it is important. History teaching sometimes suffers from the fact that its purpose is not clear either to the teacher or the children. The National Curriculum Handbook for teachers starts the history section with four quotations that give some very good reasons for teaching history. Summarised, they come down to the following points.

● History is about people; it allows us to examine the ways people behave, the ways in which they live and the things that happen to them; and it shows us that we belong to a rich tapestry of humanity.

● History is the science of story; it requires us to analyse and evaluate, to examine points of view and deduce motivation, to argue about morality and pronounce on character, all in the exciting and virtual world of the past.

● History is about identity; it shows us why the world is as it is and presents our common heritage from which we can choose the elements on which to model ourselves and the world we want to create.

● History has endless content, and it can provide high-quality material for developing literacy, artistic and musical skills and can often link strongly with other subjects in the curriculum.

The purposes of studying history at school are to:

● help understand the present in the context of the past
● arouse interest in the past
● help give children a sense of identity
● help give children an understanding of their own cultural roots and shared inheritances
● contribute to children's knowledge and understanding of other countries and other cultures in the modern world
● train the mind by means of disciplined study (history relies heavily upon disciplined enquiry, systematic analysis and evaluation, argument, logical rigour and a search for truth)
● introduce children to the distinctive methodology of historians
● enrich other areas of the curriculum
● prepare children for adult life.

Equality issues

Among the units covered in this book are the Victorians and Britain since 1930. These are particularly important because they show the development of the multicultural society in which we live today. History has tended to be Eurocentric and male-centred, but the National Curriculum has made it clear that this approach must be challenged and children's knowledge of other histories widened. This has to happen in order that children can be prepared adequately for life in the 21st century.

Through both of these units children can be encouraged to find out about the histories of their own communities and draw on this to avoid an imperialist, Eurocentric and male-centred view of the world. The movement of people is a fascinating subject in itself. Your local area may comprise a number of communities with varied heritages and languages. The Victorian era was characterised by the movement of people into the cities, and the Britain since 1930 unit covers immigration and

emigration since World War II. Local publications are often very good at taking account of 'race' and ethnicity, gender and class, and the History Channel on the television often reflects this broader approach, as do many of the websites linked to these programmes (for example www.thehistorychannel.co.uk). Unfortunately children still meet traditional and biased historical accounts in the media and in other curriculum subject areas. Some of the materials used in English lessons, for example, are rooted in history, but the 'literacy text' may be a very dated view of history. Good history teaching encourages children to challenge these narrow views of the past whenever they occur.

History and citizenship/PSHE

QCA published guidance on personal, social and health education and citizenship at the start of the millennium. A key element in this involves children learning 'to understand and respect our common humanity, diversity and differences'. History allows us to develop this understanding in a number of different ways. Studying the Aztecs involves looking at a very different type of civilisation. Many of the rituals of the Aztecs seem appalling by our standards and allow even

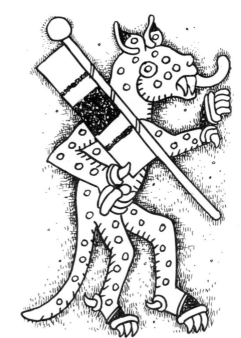

less able children to question the rules imposed by the ruling classes of the time. More able children can move on to appreciate that beliefs and values were different in the past. This can be linked to talking to parents and grandparents about what they were and were not allowed to do when they were children.

The Victorians and Britain since 1930 chapters raise other subtle questions. The introduction of the railways resulted in massive changes. Children can study this to examine causes and effects. They can use non-fiction texts to see and document what happened to individuals and groups of individuals at that time. Fictional texts can often help to explore the feelings and emotions of individuals concerned. Good historical fiction, in particular, can help children consider social and moral dilemmas because it provides a narrative context for them. They can then debate different issues and consider the consequences of choices made by individuals.

History teaching today has moved beyond teaching history as a 'march of progress', where political, social and economic aspects of life get progressively better. The great nineteenth-century historians spent little time on the failures and the experience of the marginalised or less fortunate groups such as the colonised or poor. Year 5 and 6 children can use their enquiry skills to examine wider issues than the growth of the British Empire. This can feed directly into PSHE.

Ancient Greece provides a historical framework for studying citizenship. Children who have looked at citizenship in relation to this unit tend to have quite a sophisticated understanding of the concept. They know that the term 'citizen' only applied to very specific groups and the mass of the population were excluded from the 'benefits' of citizenship. Through studying this unit, children should gain knowledge about the rights and duties of citizens and how differences existed between the city states. These are high levels of thinking skills.

History initially provides a safe context from which to explore more personal issues relating to PSHE. It teaches children to:
- look at all sides to a question or a problem and encourages them to understand that the obvious answer is not always the best one
- examine patterns in life events and make connections
- ask good and varied questions which elicit thought, such as 'How do you know that?'
- define terms – what is meant by words such as 'old', 'change'?
- clarify ideas on paper.

History and the promotion of positive attitudes

Closely linked to PSHE is the promotion of positive attitudes. School mission statements and aims often give this major priority, although there are no attainment levels in any subject which suggest looking for positive attitudes. Some schools may wish to look at this aspect of children's learning more carefully and seek to find ways in which teaching can encourage positive attitudes. History can be a key vehicle and the more independent nature of the task-setting for these four units can provide sound evidence of pupil progress and attainment.

Positive attitudes can cover all of the following.
● Enjoying learning – demonstrated by: enjoyment and enthusiasm for the topic, expressing interest in different elements of the unit, showing curiosity about the world, wanting to find out more.
● Gaining confidence/self-esteem – demonstrated by: developing confidence to use and apply knowledge gained while doing the topic, using resources to find out more, concentrating on and persevering with the task, entering sensibly into role-play situations.
● Appreciating new ideas – demonstrated by: being open-minded about learning, not always having to be right, being interested in and prepared to consider other children's views, exploring moral dilemmas, discussing a balanced viewpoint, developing an understanding and respect for others.
● Widening their application of knowledge covered in the history lesson – demonstrated by: being objective and critical of their own work, developing an awareness of the complexity of history, appreciating the role that history plays in our lives, appreciating that beliefs and values may have been different in the past.

History and ICT

Primary Foundations History: Ages 7–9 looked at six different aspects of history and ICT:
● word-processing and desktop publishing
● simulations
● databases and datafiles
● timelines
● multimedia
● the Internet.

Children who are already skilled in these areas can build on this when they do their independent research in Years 5 and 6. Many libraries have computer suites, so that children who do not have access to computers and the Internet at home can use public facilities to support their learning. History homework is often popular with children – and their parents. It promotes learning and provides plenty of opportunities for reading and writing.

If you are a newcomer looking for history sites, www.learnfree.co.uk provides a good starting point. From its initial site, click on 'Teachers'. When you reach the Teachers site, click on 'Reviews'. This gives three choices. One of these is 'Best of the Web' and this gives you access to a number of different sites which are useful for teachers.

The site www.24hourmuseum.org.uk gives direct access to museum websites and provides a fairly safe environment for children to look for museums, such as the British Museum, which provides a virtual tour of its Greek gallery. Several schools have moved into providing educational packages for other schools using sites like this and this provides an interesting move towards children creating their own ICT resources for specific audiences.

The result of children using general searches through the search engines supplied by Internet providers are varied. www.askjeeves.com.uk is a useful

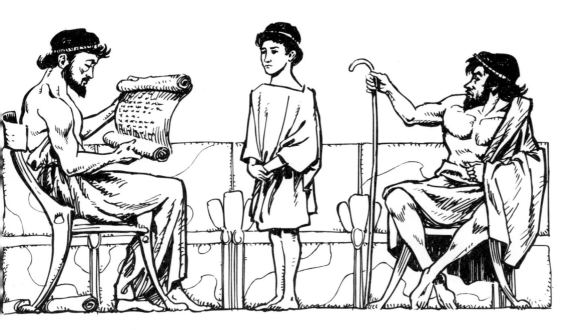

starting point, as are sites such as www.britannia.com/history which give access to quite demanding material.

A major problem in advising about the use of ICT in history is the fast pace of change. QCA History Update 2000 provides a good example of this. It has a very limited approach to using ICT in history. Yet ironically, the search for the past provides the most wonderful context for the use of this exciting medium.

History for nine- to eleven-year-olds

The teacher of nine- to eleven-year-olds has two main priorities in planning and teaching history. The first is to build on the foundations of historical knowledge, skills and understandings laid down in nursery, Key Stage 1 and the early part of Key Stage 2. The second is to ensure that progress is made in the final two years of a child's primary school career. In order to do this they need:

● good subject knowledge – books such as *Primary Foundations History* can give help with this specialist knowledge, but effective teaching requires teachers to read round the subject area and be confident about the different types of teaching strategies which can be used to enhance learning

● a good knowledge of the long-, medium- and short-term planning and teaching which has taken place prior to the children entering their class

● to ensure that their own medium- and short-term planning and teaching builds on what has taken place prior to children entering their class

● to recognise ways in which assessment and target-setting in history can be used to raise attainment across the curriculum, but particularly in literacy, because many of the skills are inter-related

● to continue to update themselves about ways in which new technology can enhance their children's learning.

Assessment

The QCA scheme of work takes a pragmatic view of assessment in history. The writers point out that their learning outcomes show how children can demonstrate what they have learnt. They then suggest that this work will serve as a record for classes working on each unit and it is not

necessary to make detailed records for each child in relation to these outcomes.

This acknowledges what most schools were already doing prior to the introduction of the QCA scheme. Assessments include the following.

● Assessment by content coverage – children are assumed to have reached the learning outcomes if they have attended the lesson and completed any task set. This is probably far the most common method of assessing history because it is so easy to manage.

● Assessment by attainment levels – the simplest way of doing this uses a checklist approach linked to the attainment levels for history. This covers each of the elements – chronological understanding; knowledge and understanding of events, people and changes in the past; historical interpretation; historical enquiry; organisation and communication. So, for Level 4 a class checklist would be like the one below.

Attainment level / Name of child						
show factual knowledge and understanding of aspects of the history of Britain and the wider world						
describe characteristic features of past societies and periods, and identify changes within and across different periods						
describe some of the main events, people and changes						
give reasons for, and results of, these events and changes						
show some understanding that aspects of the past have been represented and interpreted in different ways						
begin to select and combine information from different sources						
produce structured work, making appropriate use of dates and terms						

● Assessment through a more detailed breakdown of knowledge and skills – lesson objectives are written in this format and assessment is made for individual children on the basis of whether these objectives have been achieved. There is much to be said for breaking this down into a recording of the 'Wows' and the 'Ohs' of the lesson – recording the surprises and disappointments of individual learning.

Target-setting in history

QCA guidance includes end of unit expectations which provide broad descriptions of achievement within each unit. This allows teachers to decide whether a child's progress differs markedly from that of the rest of the class. Planning needs to be adapted if there is a systematic mismatch.

The Victorians

The Curriculum 2000 history syllabus has retained the Victorian period as an option for a modern British study unit. Its focus is on famous people and their impact on society, on changes in work and transport and the way that these changed people's lives. The following two units try to incorporate these themes. The first focuses on childhood to provide maximum interest and involvement for the children. The second looks at town life with a strong local history focus, enabling children to put into context the developments of this period. This unit also gives the opportunity for children to engage in extensive historical enquiry.

The Victorian period

The Victorian period extended from the coronation of Queen Victoria in 1837 until her death in 1901. It was the longest period in British history under one reigning monarch and marked a time of phenomenal change in all aspects of society.

Industrialisation had begun in the late 18th century, and rapidly expanded and consolidated, altering the landscape of Britain through a process of urbanisation and industrial construction and pollution. The population of Britain not only migrated from the countryside to the towns in pursuit of work, but expanded, so that by the end of the period the population had more than doubled. Following an initial phase of unrestrained development, based on a laissez-faire attitude which discouraged official control or restriction of profit-making enterprise, the Victorian period saw progressive regulation of industrial and employment practice. This stemmed from two main sources – an awakening social conscience based on issues of basic human rights and needs, and a realisation that reform would prevent severe civil unrest (represented by the beginning of the trade union and Chartist movements).

Alongside industrialisation was a dramatic entrepreneurial climate where class no longer prevented the acquisition of wealth or the emergence and flourishing of talent. Much of this 'enterprise' spirit focused upon new technologies such as steam power, especially steam-powered rail engines, automated power 'mule' weaving looms and Bessemer's steel production process. The expansion of the British Empire on the continents of Africa, Asia, Australia and into Canada opened up new and highly profitable trade markets. By the 1850s Britain was by far the wealthiest nation in the world.

At the beginning of the Victorian period, education, even at its most basic, was a lottery for the poor. Universal, compulsory free education for all children under the age of 12 was achieved in law by the end of the period (1899) though it took time to come fully into effect. Even so, most of the schools in existence today were first built and put into operation during the later Victorian period.

Many of the institutions of society as we know it stem from this period. Local government, urban public utilities, the police force, enfranchisement (at least for males), middle class moral family values and the concept of an innocent and protected childhood are just some of these. It was a period of intense confidence and national pride, revealed in many fine buildings and statuary.

Sources of evidence

Primary source evidence for this period is fairly extensive and provides an opportunity for children to look at information from different sources to answer questions and find out about the era. In addition, in almost every local community, physical evidence of the Victorians survives, for example terraces, parks, monuments and statues, schools and other public buildings such as law courts, police stations, libraries and public houses. Victorian Britain can be an exciting and enjoyable topic to teach.

Children in Victorian Britain

Pupils tend to be very interested in the lifestyles and experiences of children in times past. It is easy to harness their imagination and empathy with this topic, since the period is recent enough for children to be able to translate themselves back from their present life and empathise. The evidence is also plentiful and relatively uncomplicated, yet it stretches children, making them move beyond living memory into an abstract past. Above all, the multiple sources of evidence, often contradictory, provide rich opportunities to develop skills of synthesis and the concept of bias.

The themes of this unit include children at work, the education of children and life at home for rich and poor children. The six activity plans provide enough content for one and a half hours work each and involve using a range of primary sources as well as varied teaching and learning methods.

UNIT: Children in Victorian Britain

Enquiry questions	Learning objectives	Teaching activities	Learning outcomes	Literacy links	Cross-curricular links
What was life like for Victorian children?	● Know the dates of the Victorian period. ● Identify differences between Victorian children and today. ● Make deductions about life of Victorian children. ● Be aware of contrasting views of children and be able to give a reasoned explanation for this variation.	To establish name and dates of period. Individual sequencing on timelines. Record ideas of life then and now. Feedback. Group analysis of contrasting sources of evidence; identify what they tell us about life for Victorian children then why sources present different views; read first chapter of novel set in the period.	Children: ● know when the Victorian period was ● speculate rationally about differences between life for children then and now; ● are aware of bias in evidence concerning children in Victorian times; to be able to imagine life for Victorian children by listening to a story	Implied view from range of texts; extracts from classic writers; varied non-fiction and fiction texts with awareness of the different genres.	
What was life like for Victorian children in rich or middle class homes?	● Give features of home life for children from rich backgrounds. ● Empathise with children from this period. ● Identify differences between rich and middle class upbringings. ● Appreciate their own freedom and rights. ● Use secondary texts and ICT to answer questions about the past.	Brainstorm questions about life at home for rich children; clarify meaning of middle class, rich and poor. Provide a selection of texts and CD-ROMs for research; identify differences between rich and middle-class families; read next chapter of story or choose short story illustrating richer child's life.	● formulate questions about life for richer children in the Victorian period ● use secondary sources of information including ICT to answer questions	Locate information using contents, indexes, sections, headings, skimming, scanning and using ICT sources; to summarise, select and record key pieces of information in written form.	PSHE and citizenship: the freedom and rights of children today.
What was life like for poor Victorian children?	● Use primary sources to find out about the past. ● Empathise with poor children from the Victorian period. ● Know about Dr Barnardo.	Use primary sources to find out about poor children; summarise features of life for poor; contrast with previous lesson using display; record information about Dr Barnardo on timeline; write a short story or poem as a homeless child; read next chapter of Victorian story.	● know what life was like for Victorian poor children; know about the work of Dr Barnardo ● empathise with Victorian poor children ● extract information from range of primary visual and written sources to find out about the lives of poor children	Read various non-fiction and fiction extracts to obtain key information; to be able to write emotively either in prose or poetic forms, using expressive language.	PSHE and citizenship: value of philanthropy.
What sort of work did Victorian children do?	● Be aware of the types of jobs done by children. ● Know about Earl of Shaftesbury's social reforms. ● Construct a case study using primary and secondary sources.	Teacher input on age of children, types of work, working hours and conditions; discussion on reasons for child labour; work of Earl of Shaftesbury and key legislation; timeline; case studies of child workers; role play; read 'The Little Match Girl' by Hans Christian Andersen, or next chapter of Victorian novel.	● sequence legislation of working conditions reform on a timeline ● construct a representative and realistic case study of one child in a specific occupation	Extract information with speed from information texts; persuasive writing.	Drama: re-enact 'Little Match Girl' or act out scenes from their occupational groups. Maths: sequence numbers in chronological order.
How were children educated in Victorian times?	● Know about the different forms of schooling. ● Know when schooling became universal.	Teacher input on schooling in 1850–1900. Worksheet to test knowledge and understanding.	● know the main types of education available in 1850 and 1900 ● know the importance of the 1870 Education Act	Extracts from classic fiction describing school;	PSHE: human rights for children.
What was life like in the Victorian classroom?	● Empathise with pupils in school in the period.	Role-play Victorian classroom. Discuss feelings, impressions, differences between then and now. Draw a scene from the classroom surrounded by 'feeling' words. Read story to conclusion.	● role-play a Victorian pupil in a board school classroom ● empathise with children from the past.	Handwriting practice.	Technology: make props for Victorian classroom day. Maths: mental maths. PE: drill.

CHAPTER 1
THE VICTORIANS

Children in Victorian Britain

⏱ 1 hour 30 mins   What was life like for Victorian children?

Learning objectives
● Sequence Victorian period on a timeline.
● Interpret primary sources of information.
● Justify differing perceptions in sources.

Lesson organisation
Teacher-led input, with individual sequencing then small group work; mixed-ability group discussion then pairs; teacher-led discussion, then story.

Vocabulary
Victorian period
timeline
sources of evidence
bias

Background information

At the time of the coronation of Queen Victoria (1837) children were routinely part of the industrial, merchantile, service and agricultural workforce. Education was a luxury, usually to be paid for, or undertaken only on Sundays as part of the Sunday School Movement, but ultimately too costly in terms of time and money to be taken up by most working class families. Children were expected to earn their keep, sometimes from as early as the age of three, doing small routine piecework in the home such as making dolly pegs or matchboxes. Children were employed because of their size, their ease of submission and their cheapness. The concept that children should be protected was only just beginning to be voiced and then only in relation to extreme conditions such as working in mines or factories for excessively long hours. It was the high rate of injury and death amongst youngsters that led to reform. Much of this was exposed in Royal Commission reports into working conditions in the mines and factories. Legislation had begun to be introduced to protect children from the beginning of the century, but progress was very slow, principally because many families depended upon their children's income to keep them out of the workhouse. Parents simply lied about the age of their children and factory and mine overseers didn't question these lies. Even by the end of the century, education was only compulsory until the age of 12 years. After that it was expected that children would earn their living or be supported in fee-paying education. The continuous legislation, however, demonstrated a growing awareness of the vulnerability of children:

1802 – the Health and Morals of Apprentices Act forbade employment of children under the age of nine as apprentices and imposed a maximum working day of 12 hours for children.
1825 – the Cotton Mills Regulation Act imposed a maximum 12-hour day for workers under the age of 16 years.
1833 – the Factory Act forbade factory labour for children under nine years of age and set a nine-hour day for those under 13 years. Factory owners had to provide two hours schooling each day for child workers under 13 years (usually at the end of the working day).
1842 – the Mines Act forbade the employment of children under ten and of women below ground.
1847 – the Ten Hour Act set a ten-hour limit to the working day for women and children, with no more than 58 hours work in a week.
1864 – the Chimney Sweeps Act forbade use of children as sweeps.
1874 – no child under ten years could work in a textile mill.
1878 – all previous legislation was extended to cover all factories and workshops.

Agricultural areas continued to be free of legislative restrictions and very young children were commonly used for stone-picking, scarecrow work and harvesting. Young scullery maids were often under ten years of age and routinely worked a 14- to 16-hour day. Although the law might have distinguished the greater needs of young workers, employers frequently did not. Exploitation of young workers is still going on today.

What you need and preparation

Find a picture of Queen Victoria (large poster or on OHT), plus a story set in Victorian times (for example, Dickens' *Oliver Twist* or Kingsley's *The Water Babies*, or a modern children's novel set in the period such as Geoffrey Trease's *No Horn at Midnight*, Melvin Burgess's *The Copper Treasure*, Angela Bull's *The Winter Phantoms*), or a video (for example, *The Secret Garden* or *The Railway Children*). Prepare a class timeline and individual copies for the children, and a copy of photocopiable

sheet 93 on contrasting primary sources for each pair of children. You will also need sheets of A3 paper, and a flipchart, chalkboard or whiteboard.

What to do

(30 mins) Introduction

Show the children a picture of Queen Victoria and ask who she is and when she reigned. Write 'Queen Victoria', 'the Victorian period' and '1837–1901' on the board. Show the Victorian period on the class timeline. Give out the individual timelines for the children to block colour and label the Victorian period.

Give out an A3 sheet to each group, and ask them to brainstorm and write down the left-hand side everything they know about Victorian children's lives, then on the right-hand side what life is like for them today.

When they have finished, invite group feedback to the whole class. (This provides useful assessment of existing knowledge and misconceptions.) Highlight the key differences identified by the groups – these might include child labour, lack of education, poverty and deprivation, lack of personal rights and freedoms, physical punishment, limited toys and games. Retain these for summative assessment at the end of the unit.

(30 mins) Development

Introduce the concept of evidence by asking how can we find out about what life was like for children in the Victorian period. Lead the class to identify secondary source evidence (reference books and CD-ROMs) and primary source evidence (things written, drawn, painted or made at the time). If oral evidence is mentioned, remind the children that this period is too far back for this source, although there are transcriptions of things said by children of the time.

Ask what the Victorians thought about children. Give out copies of photocopiable page 93 to mixed-ability pairs. Explain that these contrasting sources come from a painting by a Victorian artist and the descriptions of the two children were from *Mayhew's London* first published in 1851. Explain that Henry Mayhew was a man who was concerned about the poor and who went on to the streets and slums to record what he saw of life there.

Ask the pairs what each source tells us about Victorian children. Why do they think there is such a difference between the two?

(30 mins) Plenary

Invite feedback to the whole class. Discuss the conflicting nature of the sources and the concept of bias. Why are these two sources of evidence so different? What was the artist trying to do by painting this picture? Who would buy it and put it on their walls? Would he sell a picture showing Mayhew's children? Do you think the artist was painting what he saw or what he wanted to see? Were all children like those Mayhew described? What was his purpose in describing these children?

Lead the children to understand that bias is when someone writes or paints something with a particular purpose in mind, sometimes with a particular point of view. Sources may represent life as it was for only some children, or may present an exaggerated view. The key to identifying bias is assessing the motive for producing the source of evidence.

Conclude the session by reading the first chapter of a Victorian story or showing the first part of a video.

Differentiation
Less able children could be given sticky paper cut to the right length with words and dates written on for sticking on the timelines.

Assessing learning outcomes
Can they remember and sequence the period accurately? Can they infer what lives were like for children from more than one source of evidence? Can they recognise bias and justify the contrast?

Follow-up activities
● Encourage individual research on children's lives in the Victorian period from library sources or the Internet.
● Collect Victorian art images of childhood from books or gift cards or visit an art gallery.

 # What was life like for Victorian children in rich or middle class homes?

Learning objectives
● Ask key questions about life for richer Victorian children.
● Find answers to questions using a range of secondary sources of information.
● Describe key features of home life for children from richer backgrounds.
● Understand differences between rich and middle class lives.

Lesson organisation
Teacher-led input to whole class; mixed-ability pairs engaged in research; feedback on answers to key questions, then next part of story.

Background information
Middle class and richer children's lives were undoubtedly better than those of the poorest children in terms of health and survival chances. However, life could still be grim. Freedom of choice was severely curtailed. Children were expected to follow their parents' careers and roles. Preparation began as early as possible, and aptitude and preference were irrelevant.

Children were generally kept out of sight, confined to nurseries under the care of nannies and governesses. Toys were usually plentiful but strictly controlled. In towns, outdoor activity was largely confined to a walk in the park or along the streets. Friendships were similarly vetted. At all times behaviour was expected to be adult. Punishments were frequently harsh and physical: confinement, withholding of food and corporal punishment. Relationships with parents were generally distant, the father usually playing a disciplinary role alone.

What you need and preparation
Gather as many information books on the Victorian period as possible. Include books for adults as well as children of Key Stages 1, 2 and 3. Have available CD-ROMs containing information about the Victorians. Make copies of the recording sheets on photocopiable page 94 (one between two). Provide scrap paper for note-taking, writing and drawing equipment. Have available a flipchart or board, and the next instalment of the story or video from the previous activity.

What to do
20 mins **Introduction**
Explain that the class is going to find out about life for richer children in Victorian times. Write on the board 'Rich', 'Middle class' and 'Poor'.

Ask the children to tell you what is meant by each. Stress that 'Middle class' tended to mean households of the professional classes, for example small business owners, senior clerks or stewards and shop-keepers. There would be a small household with one or two servants, probably a cook and maid of all work who helped with the cleaning and cooking (an extract from Channel 4's *The 1900 House* would help clarify the scope of the lower middle class).

Give out scrap paper and ask the children to work in pairs to think of a list of questions about life for children in rich and middle class Victorian households. Summarise the key questions on the board (for example, clothes, games, activities, food, family relationships, discipline, education, bedroom design, medicine and health).

Vocabulary
rich
middle class
poor
contents
index
subheadings

(40 mins) Development

Allocate a question each for the pairs to find the answer to, using books and CD-ROMs. Remind them of information retrieval skills, for example using contents, index and subheadings, scanning and skimming. Encourage them to concentrate on relevance to the question rather than general comments. Ask them to make rough notes, then fill in their recording sheets from photocopiable page 94, identifying the question tackled and the information discovered. Explain that this will form part of a display and should be written carefully. Illustrations can be included after the text is complete.

(30 mins) Plenary

Ask pairs to report back their findings. Summarise on the board the differences between rich and middle class children. (The middle classes tended to go to a local day school, had fewer toys but probably had a happier life with a stronger relationship with their parents.) Ask the children what it would have felt like to be a child of rich Victorian parents. Would they have liked it? Why or why not?

Read the second chapter of the Victorian story or watch a further extract of the video.

ICT opportunities
• Use CD-ROMs for information retrieval.
• Children with writing difficulties could word-process their research answers.

Follow-up activities
• Work in small groups to devise dramatic reconstructions of a rich household. Play out a scene around a key incident, such as a broken vase.
• Construct a 3-D model of a rich or middle class child's bedroom.
• Play with replica Victorian toys.

Differentiation

Assist with research for less able children, and allow those with writing difficulties to word-process their answers. Select easier secondary sources for less able children and harder, more adult, texts for children of higher ability.

Assessing learning outcomes

Can the children formulate relevant questions to direct research? Can they use secondary sources to extract information about a given question? Can they synthesise information to make general, comprehensive, accurate statements? Can they empathise with children from the past?

(1 hour 30 mins) What was life like for poor Victorian children?

Background information

Thomas Barnardo (1845–1905) was born in Ireland. He wanted to become a doctor and a missionary in China, and studied medicine at the London Hospital. Whilst there, he became greatly concerned with the plight of homeless children in the city. He became a superintendent of a ragged school in the East End, and was still a student when he opened a house for homeless boys in Stepney to give them shelter, food and education (1870). Later he opened a similar house for girls (1876). These became known as Dr Barnardo's Homes and still provide support for children in need. By Barnardo's death over 90 homes for destitute waifs had been opened under his direction. The homes were noted for their unusually high levels of care and education.

CHAPTER 1
THE VICTORIANS

Children in Victorian Britain

Learning objectives
● Use primary sources to extract information.
● Synthesise different sources to form a common understanding.
● Empathise with poor children in the Victorian period.
● Know about the contribution of Dr Barnardo to improving the lot of poor children.

Lesson organisation
Whole-class input; individual work, then feedback to whole class with teacher to summarise, then individual work; selected children to read poems, then whole class to listen to story.

Vocabulary
poor
Dr Barnardo
slum
orphan
missionary

ICT opportunities
Early finishers can use the Internet or a CD-ROM for further information on Dr Barnardo.

Follow-up activity
Research other famous Victorian reformers, including Booth, Dickens, Kingsley, Octavia Hill, Florence Nightingale, Edwin Chadwick and Joseph Lister.

Henry Mayhew was a Victorian journalist who was deeply concerned about the life of London's poor. In 1851 he published *London Labour and London Poor*, an investigation into urban poverty comprising interviews with thousands of Londoners, compiled with the help of two assistant researchers over many months. The book included testaments from pickpockets, street entertainers, flower sellers, crossing sweepers, and numerous other people, both adults and children. Ten years later, Mayhew was to publish another work, *London's Underworld*, which described the life of Victorian criminals. Mayhew's work provided some of the most useful social history of its time.

What you need and preparation
Prepare a summary of work of Dr Barnardo for a class timeline. Make copies of photocopiable page 95 (one per child). Provide writing paper, crayons and felt-tipped pens, and a computer with access to the Internet or a history CD-ROM. Have available a flipchart or board, and the next episode of the Victorian story or video.

What to do
(5 mins) Introduction
Recap on what has been found out about the lives of richer children. State that the objective of this lesson is to find out what life was like for poor children and to look at the work of two important men who helped to make life for poor children better. Introduce the names of Thomas Barnardo and Henry Mayhew.

(1 hour) Development
Distribute copies of photocopiable page 95. Explain that these extracts include some primary source evidence written during the period. Talk about the work of Henry Mayhew. Ask children to work individually to answer the questions on the worksheet.

After about 20 minutes, invite feedback and ask the children to summarise the dangers of being poor in Victorian times. Write a list on the board. Include hunger, cold, illness, overcrowding, excessive work, violence and bullying, freedom to roam (accidents), ignorance. Contrast this with the previous lesson's work and identify the differences in conditions.

Talk about the work of Dr Barnardo, recording key information on the board with labels to be placed on a class timeline. Then invite the children to write a short story or poem in the first person from the viewpoint of a homeless child out on the streets one freezing night who is rescued by Dr Barnardo. Ask them to write their story or poem in two parts – feelings and description of life on the street and feelings and life after rescue. Once the composition is complete, let them add illustrations.

(25 mins) Plenary
Read selected extracts from the children's work, then read the next chapter of the story or show the next 15 minutes of the video.

Differentiation
Less able children could write their story in cartoon format – two pictures of before and two after. Assist less able children with the worksheet by using only one source.

More able children could do further research into the work of Mayhew and Barnardo.

Assessing learning outcomes

Can the children extract and synthesise information about the lives of the poor from primary sources? Can they write a story or poem that shows that they can empathise with poor children in the Victorian period?

What sort of work did Victorian children do?

Background information

Anthony Ashley Cooper, Earl of Shaftesbury (1801–1885) was an upper class landowner, who worked in Parliament to reform working conditions for children and women and to ban the use of children in mines and restrict their hours of work in factories. He believed it was his religious and moral duty to help the poor. He entered Parliament in 1826 and worked tirelessly for reform during the 1830s and 1840s, during which time the Ten Hour Act (1847) and the Mines Act (1842) were passed. The Mines Act banned the employment of children under ten and women underground in mines. The Ten Hour Act set the limit for working hours for women and children to ten hours a day and no more than 58 hours a week (our current maximum working week for adults is 48 hours).

He was also a patron of ragged schools – free after-work schools for the poor. He was said to have begged for money for these schools from his fellow MPs as they went in and out of the Houses of Parliament. In the 39 years of operation the Ragged Schools Union allowed close to 300,000 destitute children to be educated free. Shaftesbury also established soup kitchens where the hungry could get free meals.

What you need and preparation

Collect information on Lord Shaftesbury, the 1842 Mine Act, the 1847 Ten Hour Act, and work conditions and types of work done by Victorian children. Prepare labels for Lord Shaftesbury and the two Acts to go on the class timeline, and provide access to the children's individual timelines. Provide information books on Victorian Britain for the children to use, and copies of photocopiable pages 96 to 98 (one between two).

What to do

Introduction

20 mins Start by asking the children if any of them have paid jobs. Call for examples and reasons for doing the work. Talk about the types of jobs done by children in the Victorian period. These could include domestic service, factory work, mining (early in the period), apprenticeships, shop work, chimney sweeps, stone-pickers, crow-scarers and crop-pickers, crossing sweepers, scavengers, match-box makers, glove makers, washing peg makers, sewing, button makers (see extracts from photocopiable pages 96 and 97). Some of the jobs, such as crow-scaring or stone-picking, might require explanation. (Why don't we need to do these jobs today?) Talk about the age of the children and their working conditions – excessive hours and temperatures, limited or no breaks, bullying and physical punishment by employers or overseers, sickness and occupational accidents and injury, stunting of growth, damage to eyesight and lungs, robbery and cruelty.

Ask the children to discuss in groups of four to six why they think children worked in these conditions and jobs.

With the whole class, summarise the main points. Children worked because they had to – they and their families would have starved if they had not; there were no benefits, medical care or free schooling; there was an expectation that children would work as early as from the age of three to contribute to their own keep. Point out that things were changing and many social reformers were campaigning for the restriction and banning of child labour.

Learning objectives

• Be aware of the types of jobs done by children.
• Understand why children had to work.
• Know of the work of Lord Shaftesbury in relation to child labour reform.

Lesson organisation

Whole-class teacher-led input, with mixed-ability group discussion and feedback; mixed-ability pairs working on research; selected pairs to give an exposition to the class.

Children in
Victorian
Britain

Vocabulary
apprentice
stone-pickers
domestic service
mudlark
Ten Hour Act
Lord Shaftesbury

Development

45 mins Talk about the work of the Earl of Shaftesbury and the two key pieces of legislation he managed to get through Parliament despite opposition from merchants and factory and mine owners. Talk about how children were cheap sources of labour, often being paid a fraction of the adult rate. They were plentiful, easily controlled and bullied, and their small size made them very valuable for cleaning or operating in tight spaces such as low tunnels, under machinery and up chimneys. Point out how parents also opposed these reform acts where they could because they needed their children to bring in a wage.

Get the children to record on their individual timelines the dates of Lord Shaftesbury and his two Acts. Put labels on the class timeline.

Explain that the children are going to work in pairs to prepare a fictional profile of a working Victorian child of their own age using photocopiable pages 96 and 97 and/or information books and the computer sources for information, then writing up the profile on the worksheet from photocopiable page 98. Suggested jobs could include: chimney sweep (boy), scullery maid or stable boy for a rich family, mine worker (boy), apprentice (boy), factory worker, home worker, stone-picker, crow-scarer or crop picker. Allow a choice of jobs but try to get a full coverage of all occupations.

Plenary

25 mins Take on the role of Lord Shaftesbury and ask selected children to role-play giving 'evidence' to the Commission of Child Labour. Call children up to stand before you in turn and answer in role. Ask them detailed questions about their jobs. (What is your name? What job do you do? How many hours do you work a day? Tell me what you do each day? What is the worst part of your work?)

Reiterate the reasons children worked in Victorian times and why nowadays children are neither allowed nor generally forced to work to live. Point out that much of that freedom comes from the legislation pushed through by Lord Shaftesbury and his fellow reformers.

Differentiation

Assist less able readers, helping to direct them to appropriate passages for use in the case study or use the previously discussed source from photocopiable pages 96 and 97.

More able children could be asked to looked at two contrasting types of work done by children, one urban (for example factory worker) and one agricultural (for example crop picker). Which would they prefer and why? Were there any jobs that were common to both town and country?

Follow-up activities
• Invite children to do art work based on a scene from the child profile.
• Let small groups re-enact scenes from the child's life.
• Read 'The Little Match Girl' by Hans Christian Andersen and dramatise it or do creative writing from it.

Assessing learning outcomes

Can the children speculate reasonably about why Victorian children worked? Can they construct an accurate profile of a child labourer and demonstrate an understanding of working conditions through role-play in character? Can they record accurately on a timeline the dates related to the work of Lord Shaftesbury?

How were children educated in Victorian times?

Background information

At the beginning of the Victorian period, schooling was a matter of chance or funding. The Sunday School Movement had led to Sunday education for children in basic numeracy and literacy, RE and practical work skills such as gardening or coarse needlework. Sometimes this education was free. Factories were expected to provide schooling for their apprentices, but where enlightened factory owners made the effort to comply with legislation, pupils no doubt struggled to stay awake having worked all day.

The middle and working classes paid to send their children to grammar schools, church schools, dame schools, or monitorial schools. Rich children were educated at home by tutors and governesses, or at public school (boys only). Boys were often sent to fee-paying boarding schools or to grammar schools. Here the curriculum was largely based on the classical model of Latin, Greek, arithmetic, astronomy, philosophy and rhetoric. Occasionally boys were educated by private tutors at home. Girls were educated by governesses mostly, in literacy and housekeeping accounting, but also in 'womanly' arts such as music, dancing, needlework, art and foreign languages.

In 1861 a committee was established to consider education for the poor that was both cheap and good quality. Its report (1862) recommended the introduction of a Revised Code of Standards with payment by results and universal provision (although not free) for children between the ages of five and ten years. The final recommendation was enshrined in the Foster Education Act of 1870. Lord Howe in his report on the education of the poor recommended that a fixed curriculum be implemented in reading, writing and arithmetic to make sure standards were maintained in schools funded by government grants and also that education be universally available to all children. The Revised Code came into operation in 1862 with inspectors visiting schools annually to test children and check attendance figures then pay teachers for those who had passed the levels and attended regularly (payment by results). In 1880 an Act made schooling compulsory to ensure children had the opportunity to be educated, but it wasn't until 1891 that schooling was made free, and the age of leaving raised simultaneously to 11. Many children still worked outside school hours to provide for the family.

In 1870, after much dispute, the Education Act was passed under the control of Foster. It allowed for universal education to become a reality for children between five and ten years of age, although parents had to pay for children to attend school. Local Education Boards were set up to build and run the new so-called 'Board Schools'.

By 1901 the age of attendance at school had been raised to 12; it was compulsory and it was free to all. Still many children failed to attend or attended only sporadically, despite punishment for

Learning objectives
● Know about the types of schooling available in the Victorian period.
● Understand the importance of the 1870 Education Act.
● Know what sort of curriculum was practised in Board Schools.

Lesson organisation
Teacher-led input to whole class and individual work throughout.

Vocabulary
Foster Education Act
dame schools
governesses
ragged schools
Sunday schools
Board Schools
curriculum
punishment book

ICT opportunities
Let children search CD-ROMs for information on Victorian schooling.

absence. Most were having to work (illegally), while others were too sick or had to mind younger children at home. Nevertheless by this time the principle that all children had a right to be educated had been established.

By the end of the period, education was of a higher quality and far more widely available. It was a mixture of pragmatism and idealism that brought this about. New technologies required a literate and numerate workforce. At the same time Matthew Arnold, amongst others, was proposing that education was a human right that should be the entitlement of all within a civilised society. This is now taken for granted but would have been considered a rather strange ideology at the beginning of the 19th century.

What you need and preparation

Do plenty of background reading and find background information on education in 1850 and 1900 and the impact of the Foster Education Act 1870. Provide writing materials, information books with illustrations of life in school, labels for the Education Act (1870) for the class timeline. Find either a copy of Charlotte Bronte's *Jane Eyre* or a video of the film, and have the school scene at hand. Obtain Victorian schoolroom props, such as a cane, stool, dunce's hat, sign saying 'idiot', slate and slate pencil and ink pen. Prepare copies of photocopiable pages 99 (extracts from a school log book) and 100 (a worksheet) for each child. Have ready the next instalment of the Victorian story or video.

What to do

10 mins Introduction

Ask the children about the features of education today (compulsory for five- to 16-year-olds, a National Curriculum, no physical punishment of pupils). Why do we have this compulsory education for children (their right to be educated, to improve their prospects of employment and to be protected from harm)?

Make the point that for well over half of the Victorian period very few children had any sort of education. Many were illiterate and had to work all day. Education cost money, either in lost wages or payment for schooling. Ask the children to recollect the name of any types of schooling available for children in the Victorian period (for example ragged schools, governesses).

1 hour Development

Talk about education in the mid-19th century. Show pictures from information books illustrating the types of schools available. Talk about the Foster Education Act of 1870 and discuss its impact.

Show the children a video of the school scene from *Jane Eyre* or read an extract from the book itself. Tell the children that this is set in a Victorian board school. Talk about how discipline in all schools was very harsh by today's standards – canes, straps and rulers were used to maintain order. (Show the children the cane.) The curriculum was learned largely by repetition and constant practice. There was no talking or discussion in class and no play time. Show the children the dunce's hat, the stool and the sign, which would have been placed around the offender's neck. Explain that the point was to humiliate.

Show the extracts from the log book on photocopiable page 99 and talk about the curriculum then and now. What are the similarities and differences? Explain how children learned the '3Rs', religion and drill (physical exercises at their desks). Talk about the school log book as shown on the photocopiable page. Show the slate, charcoal pencil, ink and ink pen and invite the children to try them out.

Give out copies of the worksheet on photocopiable page 100 and ask children to work through the questions.

Follow-up activities

• Let the children make simple pinafores or mop caps (girls) or flat caps (boys) for role-play.

• Look at some of the moral tales and mottoes used in school and question their purpose (moral development). Suitable examples are: spare the rod and spoil the child; waste not want not; cleanliness is next to godliness; the wages of sin is death; God sees everything.

• Make some needlework samplers.

• Investigate the history of your own school and look at any surviving evidence of Victorian times.

20 mins **Plenary**
Conclude with a brief discussion on what it would have been like to have this type of education every day. Include your own impressions. Read the last part of the Victorian story or watch the conclusion of the video. Tell the children that in the next lesson they will be re-enacting life in a Victorian classroom and that they will be expected to dress and act accordingly!

Differentiation
Less able children can have access to information texts to help them to the answer the questions on the worksheet.

More able children can be encouraged to undertake further research about Victorian schooling methods for later presentation to the rest of the class.

Assessing learning outcomes
Can the children recall and record information about schools and legislation from the Victorian period? Can the children identify the differences between schooling then and now?

1 hour 30 mins What was life like in the Victorian classroom?

Background information
Discipline in all Victorian schools was very harsh by modern standards, with canes, straps and rulers being routinely used to keep order. Humiliation was another commonplace disciplinary procedure, with children being made to stand in the corner or on a stool, often wearing a dunce's cap or having a sign saying 'stupid' or 'idiot' hung round their neck. Lessons were learned largely by repetition and constant practice.

What you need and preparation
Brief children and parents well in advance about the role-play activity, getting children to wear appropriate costume as far as possible. Prepare the classroom by arranging chairs and tables in rows, with a central front teacher's desk, preferably raised on a platform or stage blocks, and remove any attractive displays. If available, obtain a cane, a dunce's stool and cap, ink pens, slates and slate pencils, a globe and a replica map of the British Empire. Prepare a Victorian-type costume for yourself. Write a few maths sums on the board, plus today's date (but 100 years earlier) in joined-up writing. Prepare copies of photocopiable page 101 for each child, and provide plain and lined paper and colouring pencils. Brief a couple of children to act as a 'dunce' and a naughty child who is to be caned. Remind them to respond appropriately!

What to do
10 mins **Introduction**
Remind children about what they have found out so far about life in the Victorian

Learning objectives
• Empathise with children in a Victorian board school.
• Role-play with accuracy the behaviour of a Victorian schoolchild.

Lesson organisation
Teacher-led input to whole class and individual work throughout.

Vocabulary
drill
arithmetic
3-Rs
slate
dunce

classroom. Tell them that for the next hour they will act as Victorian schoolchildren. Remind them that they must sit up in their rows with backs straight, keeping silent unless you speak to them, and standing up to answer a question.

Development

1 hour Begin with prayers for the safety of Queen Victoria and the expansion of the British Empire. Take a register, with each child standing when answering.

Spend a few minutes chanting the multiplication tables, then give the class some mental maths questions. Stress that there must be no speaking out of turn. Appoint a monitor to hand out paper, then get the children to answer the maths questions on the board. Stress that the work must be neat and that crossings-out will be punished! Again, remind them that they are not allowed to talk to each other.

Appoint a 'monitor' to hand out the copying exercises on photocopiable page 101. Allow the children 20 minutes or so to work through it. Stress the importance of neatness and point out that in Victorian times messiness would have been severely punished. While they are working, patrol up and down the rows, tapping the cane menacingly on your hand. At an appropriate moment call out the pre-briefed 'actors' and administer the appropriate punishments. The 'caning' should take place out of sight, and the child encouraged to respond appropriately.

Finally try some drill practice. Get the children to stand with arms out straight, then overhead, then out at side. Repeat this 15 times. Get them to bend their knees, straighten them, stand on tiptoe then down (again 15 times). Stress that there should be no slouching or talking, but sharp precision of movement. Explain that this was sometimes done standing on benches or stools to ensure concentration. Drill outside involved marching and jumping in rows and columns.

Conclude your Victorian lesson with the children standing and singing 'God Save the Queen' or the chorus of 'Rule Britannia', then prayers and finally chanting 'Good morning/afternoon, Miss/ Sir'.

Plenary

20 mins If possible, allow the children five minutes play outside to let off stress, while you return the classroom to normal.

Give out plain paper and ask the children to draw a scene from the classroom and surround it with 'feeling' words. Allow them to discuss their experience as they work.

Differentiation
Make sure that the maths questions are within reach of less able children.

Only the children of higher ability should be asked the more difficult questions to avoid humiliation.

Assessing learning outcomes
Can the children role-play the life of pupils in a Victorian schoolroom? Are they able to empathise with Victorian children?

Follow-up activities
● Re-enact the Victorian classroom scene for parents.
● Encourage creative writing about the children's experiences in the Victorian classroom.

Victorian towns and town life

This unit aims to incorporate local history elements into a study of urban development and public service and utility provision. Railway and other transport provision has been included.

In 1851 the census recorded that the population of England and Wales was approximately 18 million. Of that number 50 per cent was concentrated in urban areas. By the end of the period (1901) the population had grown to over 32 million and the urban population had increased to 77 per cent.

Most towns have numerous examples of Victorian housing, ranging from large villas to terraced houses, which can provide great scope for a history trail. In addition most towns have examples of Victorian factories, warehouses or dockland developments that were proud architectural statements of the commercial enterprises of the time. During this period, local authorities began to pull down private slum housing and many engaged in substantial urban planning projects designed to improve the environment. Impressive town halls, public libraries, art galleries, street lighting, paving, public infirmaries and dispensaries testify to the importance of these august bodies.

Schools also survive, usually bearing a foundation stone and a date. Public buildings available for study also include churches (of all denominations), police stations, public baths and technical colleges.

Monuments frequently stem from this period, for example, statues and war memorials to the Crimean and Boer Wars. Public parks often originate from this time and may have remaining palm houses or wrought iron gates. All this provides easily available physical evidence of the contribution of the Victorian period to urban development and infrastructure.

UNIT: Victorian towns and town life

Enquiry questions	Learning objectives	Teaching activities	Learning outcomes	Literacy links	Cross-curricular links
How did towns develop during the Victorian period?	• Identify Victorian buildings and artefacts from local environment. • Know about the extent of expansion of local community during Victorian period. • Identify reasons for urban expansion. • Identify nature and extent of change from comparable sources of evidence.	Field walk round area to look at Victorian legacy. Look at other types of evidence for Victorian influence in local area.	Children: • use maps, directories and photographs to chart change in a town • make comparisons across two or three different fixed time points • know that towns generally expanded in population and industry during the Victorian period	Extract information from lists.	Maths: data handling. Geography: extract information from maps/urban formation.
What were the housing and public health problems during the Victorian period?	• Know what housing was like for the poorest and richest families. • Know how to use the census and local descriptions to find out about housing. • Imagine what it was like to live in poor and richer houses. • Know the key public health reforms from this period.	Research into poor housing, reading contemporary accounts. Investigate census records	• use census sources to find out about over-crowding • know that over-crowding existed in smaller towns as well as cities • know about the problems resulting from urban over-crowding and the solutions designed to tackle the problems	Extract information from different non-fiction texts.	Geography: large-scale map of poorer and richer areas in locality.
How did people get about in the Victorian towns?	• Know what sorts of transport were available to the Victorians. • Know about transport advances of the period. • Recreate a debate concerning the coming of the railway. • Understand the advantages and disadvantages of the arrival of the railway. • Appreciate different points of view existed about transport advances.	Research into Victorian transport in the locality. Design a transport poster. Debate the advantages and disadvantages of the coming of the railway.	• identify transport systems available to a local community in the Victorian period • use primary sources of evidence to find out about local transport • know the transport advances of the period and their dates during the period • understand different points of view over coming of railway		Art: poster design. PSHE: citizenship (debate and voting).
What help was given to the poor in towns?	• Know the types of official and voluntary provision for the poor in towns. • Understand attitudes to the poor, particularly the concepts of 'laissez faire', 'self-help' and the 'deserving' poor. • Imagine what it would have been like to be a child in a workhouse.	Define 'the poor'. Look at attitude of Scrooge in *A Christmas Carol*. Research work of Salvation Army and other organisations that developed during the period. Empathise with people in workhouse.	• imagine life for children in the workhouse and write a descriptive and emotive piece on this • know the types of provision for the poor likely to be available at town level • understand the attitudes to the poor that were prevalent in the Victorian period • know the key dates of the foundation of the police service • are aware of common crimes and sentencing policy in the Victorian period	Creative writing. Read for meaning from non-fiction and fiction texts. Understand motives for fictional texts and characters.	PSHE: empathy towards poorer children.
How did the Victorians deal with crime?	• Know the history of the police foundation and its progress during the period. • Know the sort of penalties for crime. • Understand that in the early part of the period children committing crimes faced the full rigour of the law. • Write a newspaper report of a crime and trial for an offence occurring in their local town.	Investigate and discuss crimes and sentences. Make comparisons with today. Worksheet and writing own newspaper account.	• know the key reforms to law and order during the period • are able to write a fictional newspaper report for a crime and trial, set locally.	Write in journalistic style. Newspaper reports.	

 # How did towns develop during the Victorian period?

Background information

People were attracted to towns by offers of work and better wages. However, it was not always a better life in the towns, and hard times often resulted from being laid off, lock-outs and very low wages when trade was hit by economic downfalls and increased competition from abroad, particularly grain imports from America. This hardship, combined with a strictly profit-led business management, spawned the birth of the Trade Union Movement, illegal for much of this period, and the Chartist Movement (1840s), designed to increase the electoral rights of the working class and improve basic human rights.

Urbanisation resulted in the best and worst of worlds. Poverty was more extreme because of the appalling living conditions and lack of agricultural plots where the poor labourer could grow food or rear animal stock. Nor could the urban poor easily forage for wood to burn for fuel. Families had to buy all the essential foodstuffs. This left them critically dependent upon their wages and led to frequent reliance on the pawn shop and loan sharks, so much a feature of Dickens' novels.

What you need and preparation

Devise a local history trail, taking in examples of Victorian buildings, monuments and parks. Enlist the support of adult assistants. Have available a camcorder or camera and film. Prepare a map of the trail and photocopy it for each child to record the buildings and physical evidence looked at on the trail, and prepare differentiated worksheets asking questions about what the children observe during the field work. Make an enlarged copy of the map for display. Organise children into groups by ability. Have available some old photos of the town, and have one or two of them enlarged for whole-class use, and take some photos of comparable sites and buildings now. If possible collect some OS maps (6 inches to the mile) of the locality from the beginning, middle and end of the period to show expansion or change (the outer limits of the town or railway areas often show this best). Prepare copies of photocopiable page 102 (a three-column chart to record comparative information from directories) for groups of average ability and page 103 (a worksheet for recording expansion pictorially) for children of higher ability. Make photocopies of extracts from commercial directories of your town for two or preferably three periods. Provide lined paper, and have available a flipchart or board.

What to do

10 mins Introduction

Discuss the purpose and demands of the field walk. Distribute the worksheets and recording sheets.

2 hours Development

Spend about 50 minutes taking the children on their field walk. Encourage them to look for as much evidence as they can find for the Victorian influence on your locality.

Back in the classroom, mark on your large map the Victorian buildings and monuments in the locality using the children's observations.

Show the enlarged photograph of the Victorian street scene. Ask the children to identify changes in the buildings or streets, including change of use based on observations made on the field walk and on the photographic evidence from the modern pictures.

Tell the class that they are going to find out about how the town changed during the period and between then and now. Explain that three sources of evidence will be used – photographs, street directories and maps.

Learning objectives
● Observe Victorian buildings and infrastructure surviving in present local environment.
● Identify differences in towns then and now using photographic evidence.
● Chart growth and change to the locality during the Victorian period using directories and maps.
● Know that during the Victorian period there was substantial urban development.

Lesson organisation
Whole-class teacher-led input; small groups with adult assistance for field work, then children work in pairs but with individual recording; whole-class feedback and teacher input.

Vocabulary
change
institute
monuments
urban
directories
Ordnance Survey

Victorian
towns and
town life

Split the class into three groups. The less able children should reinforce the work done using photographic evidence. Provide them with copies of the Victorian photographs for comparison with the contemporary examples to identify changes between then and now. Direct them with specific questions if appropriate. (What was this building used for then and now? How has this street changed from the Victorian period to now?) Ask them to record their answers on paper.

Children of average ability can work on commercial directories, comparing population lists and numbers of businesses and types (for example, number of inns or public houses, shops, schools). Give them copies of photocopiable page 102 for recording their evidence. Ask them to write up a conclusion: in what ways did the town change in the Victorian period?

Children of higher ability can work on Ordnance Survey maps, comparing them first with a modern map of a similar scale, then with different periods during the Victorian era or just after. Encourage them to look for evidence of change and chart it on the three-block record sheet on photocopiable page 103. Ask them to conclude by answering the question: in what ways did the town expand during the Victorian period?

20 mins Plenary

Invite representatives from the three groups to report back to the class about changes to the town during the Victorian period and between then and now. Summarise the changes and talk about expansion of towns throughout the country, linking local with national development.

Differentiation

Children of lower ability should be given a differentiated worksheet for use on the field trip with specially tailored questions. Give them additional support as necessary when working with the photographic sources.

Children of higher ability have their own differentiated task and should be encouraged to carry out independent research.

Assessing learning outcomes

Can the children observe and record Victorian physical evidence in the town? Can they chart change during the period and between then and now, using two or more of the same sources from different time points? Can they draw conclusions about comparative evidence and synthesise this with other sources?

ICT opportunities

• Information from directories can be keyed into a database.
• Photos and maps can be scanned in for storage and individual work, and overlays of maps can be provided to make changes explicit.

Follow-up activities

• Do further work on directories to chart occupational change.
• Undertake art and technology work on the construction of a Victorian street, based on photographic evidence, maps and observation.

 # What were the housing and public health problems during the Victorian period?

Background information

Urbanisation brought with it severe public health problems with frequent epidemics of cholera, dysentery and typhus, spread mainly by contaminated water supplies. Bad water supplies affected every level of society, but amongst the overcrowded, malnourished and weakened urban poor, its toll was catastrophic. Edwin Chadwick's reports into public health (1842) and on sanitation (1848) led to vital subsequent legislation and shocked Members of Parliament and the literate liberal classes. It was reported that the average life expectancy at that time for a Manchester worker was 17 years of age. This compared with a rural life expectancy of 33 years for labourers. By the 1880s life expectancy in towns for workers had risen to 30 years and was 53 years in the country. This was largely due to public health reforms, with the construction of public sewers and free piped water supplies, aided by employment conditions legislation.

Most of the oldest housing around today is Victorian in date, especially in market towns or cities. Slums virtually disappeared in the slum clearance programmes of the late Victorian and the post-World War II period. The terraced house remains the strongest Victorian survival but villa houses and big semi-detached and detached properties belonging to the middle classes also survive in sufficient numbers to be common. There are also larger mansions with their own drives and walled gardens, many of which have now been converted into nursing homes, flats or business premises.

What you need and preparation

Try to obtain photographs of local houses taken during the Victorian period. Alternatively, obtain reference books showing all kinds of Victorian housing, from the richest to the poorest. Transcribe some Victorian census material (available from your local library or public records office) for the richer, the middle class and the poorest streets from your local community. These should all be from the same decade if possible. Make an OHT of the largest scale Victorian OS map possible, showing courts or back-to-back housing in your locality. Have available information about Edwin Chadwick and his Public Health Reforms. Prepare copies of photocopiable pages 104 and 105, so that the children can have one between two. Provide paper or exercise books, Victorian OS maps of the locality and labels for class timeline for Chadwick and his Public Health Acts.

What to do

15 mins Introduction

Explain the objective of lesson – to find out about the types of housing in the locality that people lived in during the Victorian period and to find out about some of the problems that came from rapid urban development.

Talk about the general types of housing found during the period (if possible using illustrations and photographs from the local community). Describe rich housing (large houses and grounds, with servants), middle class housing (detached and semi-detached housing), working class housing (terraces with back courtyards and outside latrines) and finally the poorest type of housing (courts and back-to-back with communal latrines and no water other than a street pump or a stream). Show pictures of each if possible.

70 mins Development

Read the extract from Mrs Gaskell's *Mary Barton* on photocopiable page 104. Point out that it was written in the 1840s and was set in Manchester. Ask the children to imagine what it would

Learning objectives
● Know about the types of poor and richer Victorian housing.
● Understand that rapid urbanisation and lack of regulation produced areas of very poor housing, with over-crowding, disease and deprivation.
● Know about the reforms in public health instituted by Edwin Chadwick.
● Be able to use census material to compare different types of households.

Lesson organisation
Whole class, with teacher-input; whole class, then pairs and individuals; whole class, with teacher-input and questioning.

Vocabulary
courts
back-to-back housing
sewers
pollution
cellars
terrace
villa
dysentery
cholera
typhoid
typhus

have been like to live there in the cellar. Why are the family living there? What are the problems of living in a cellar?

Explain how poor housing came about, with rapidly built homes, no piped water supply or sewage drainage, just open sewers with shared latrines draining into them. Talk about how poor families were obliged to live in one room, sometimes sharing with other families. Ask the children to read the extract on photocopiable page 105 which gives a statistical report of poor housing in the period. Ask them to work through the questions.

After about 25 minutes, split the class into three groups. Ask them to work in pairs within their groups. Explain that they are going to look at the census records and investigate a particular street and identify the type of area it was in, for example poor, middle class or richer. Explain the format of census records and their purpose if the children are unfamiliar with them (by street and house, listing names details about the occupants).

Hand out the prepared transcripts of census material for the three social classes. OS maps from earlier work should be available for additional research if required. Ask the pairs to take notes on anything in the transcripts that might suggest the nature of the housing. Explain that they will report back later to the whole class about their findings.

Pairs who finish early can prepare a short dialogue between two children who come from the street they have been investigating, one a newcomer, one who has lived there a long time. The newcomer can ask questions about the area.

Spend a few minutes inviting pairs to give feedback to the whole class about the types of housing and where they are. Use the large-scale map to show locations. Allow a few enactments of dialogues, one from each type of area if possible.

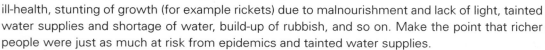
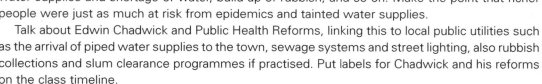

Talk about the problems arising from poor housing – over-crowding; spread of diseases (for example cholera, typhoid, influenza, dysentery, scarlet fever), ill-health, stunting of growth (for example rickets) due to malnourishment and lack of light, tainted water supplies and shortage of water, build-up of rubbish, and so on. Make the point that richer people were just as much at risk from epidemics and tainted water supplies.

Talk about Edwin Chadwick and Public Health Reforms, linking this to local public utilities such as the arrival of piped water supplies to the town, sewage systems and street lighting, also rubbish collections and slum clearance programmes if practised. Put labels for Chadwick and his reforms on the class timeline.

⑤ Plenary
mins Recap on the types of housing people lived in during the Victorian period, the problems and solutions. Use questioning to assess knowledge and understanding.

Differentiation
More able children can work on more challenging original sources, and less able children should have more teacher support. If appropriate, organise work in mixed-ability pairs to facilitate learning.

Assessing learning outcomes
Can the children assimilate census evidence to identify a type of housing in the local community? Can they empathise with children living in different conditions?

**ICT
opportunities**
• Put census records on the computer for ease of storage and access.
• Use of database analysis might be possible.

**Follow-up
activities**
• Recreate families from the census (poor, richer and middle class).
• Creative writing, drama, art and house construction in technology are all possible from this research.

 # How did people get about in Victorian towns?

Background information

In 1837 transporting goods and people was possible by road though only by horse-drawn vehicles. Coaches plied the roads paying tolls on turnpike stretches, delivering people and post. Richer folk owned their own carriages and hansom cabs were available for hire. Canals shipped freight and passengers. Ferries and ships coursed the rivers and seas. The railway was just beginning. Most people, however, did not travel further than they could walk.

By 1901 the rail network was extensive, there were horseless carriages and buses, electric trams and omnibuses on the streets of the cities. London had its own underground railway. Many more people travelled long distances. Grid-lock was common, and accidents were frequent.

Perhaps the most major innovation of this period was the establishment of the railway network. Designed to facilitate trade and transfer of goods, it ended up altering the whole way of life of the population, from the supply of fresh produce to markets in city centres, to the development of suburbia where commuting to work became an option for the middle classes.

What you need and preparation

Locate some primary source material about Victorian transport in your locality. Obtain copies of town directories, large-scale OS town maps showing a railway, copies of a local newspaper, and photographs of local Victorian street scenes, enough for one example per group of six. Make copies of photocopiable page 106 for each child, and provide an A3 grid for recording transport type from primary source analysis (one per group of six), felt-tipped pens, plain scrap paper for poster design, and a computer with CD-ROM information on the Victorians. You will also need access to a board or flipchart.

What to do

5 mins Introduction

Explain that you are going to look at transport in Victorian times, particularly in your locality. Ask the children about transport choices available today to, from and within their town or area. List these on one side of the board. Make sure you include walking and driving.

80 mins Development

Split the class into ability groups of about six. Tell them that they are going to spend about 35 minutes identifying and recording the types of transport available in the community in Victorian times using a range of sources of evidence, such as street directories, newspapers, OS maps and photographs. Supply each group with one A3 sheet to record the types of transport they have found and from which source of information it came.

When the task is completed, let the children work individually to design an advertisement poster for a Victorian local transport system based on the evidence they have found (mode of transport, appearance, route, price, and so on). This can be developed and completed later in art.

Compile a class list of types of Victorian transport. Invite less able children to give their feedback first. Add walking and horse-riding if they have not been mentioned. Ask the class questions about the similarities and differences in transport between then and now.

Explain that there were many innovations and advances in transport made during the Victorian period. Give out the transport quiz sheet on photocopiable page 106. Emphasise that this is just a game. They must work individually and try to guess which invention was made and when by matching dates to types of transport. After completion, they can confer with their neighbours and compare results.

Feed back to the whole class by giving the right answers on the board and adding information about inventors and early models. Then let the children record the advances in the right place on the timeline on the bottom of the photocopiable sheet (railway 1830s; horse-drawn buses 1830s; underground trains 1860s; bicycle late 1880s; electric trams 1890s; cars 1890s). Early finishers can extend their timeline by adding 20th century transport advances with speculative dates (motor buses and coaches, planes, space travel, hovercraft). Alternatively, they could use the CD-ROM to research a particular form of transport.

Talk about the dramatic expansion of the railway during the 1830–40s. Ask for suggestions concerning the advantages of having the railway come to the town. Then ask for any disadvantages. If they have trouble with ideas, tell the children about effects on the local people, such as compulsory purchase orders without compensation, destruction of housing and countryside, the impact of the crowds, danger to livestock and people, the rapid change and increase in industry.

Split the class into four groups and tell them that they are going to represent different people involved in a debate about the benefits of the coming of the railway: those for, those against, those undecided and the railway company representatives. Give the groups five minutes to come up with a good argument and elect two spokespersons to voice that view. The 'undecided' group should talk about the issues amongst themselves but elect two people to ask questions of the other groups. Organise a formal debate with proposers, for and against, each allowed three minutes to speak. Then the 'undecided' group should be allowed five minutes to ask questions to the proposers.

5 mins Plenary

Ask the children to cast their votes for or against the new railway. Record the results and their decision whether to allow the railway to come or not.

Differentiation

Lower-ability groups should work on just the photographs and directories. Give them structured support and implicit instructions on organisation and a specific task. (You two look at this newspaper and see if you can find any mention or pictures of transport, write down what you find, and then we'll put it on the big sheet later.)

Give groups of average ability access to all sources excluding the maps. Suggest that they pair off to examine one source then feed back to the whole group for recording.

Allow more able children access to all sources, but do not help in the organisation of the task.

Assessing learning outcomes

Can the children extract relevant information from a range of sources concerning transport? Can they complete a timeline of transport advances accurately? Can they enter into a debate by summarising arguments and asking appropriate questions?

**ICT
opportunities**
Encourage research work on transport using a CD-ROM.

Follow-up activities
● Children can complete the transport poster in art.
● Ask the children to write a newspaper article on the public debate.
● Children could search old local newspapers for controversy surrounding the coming of the railway to their own town.
● Research different transport systems for inventors and models.

What help was given to the poor in towns?

Background information

Many hospitals began their work in the Victorian period, and public infirmaries would often take non-paying patients as an act of charity. Several modern hospitals started life as workhouses. An act of parliament in 1928 converted all existing workhouses into infirmaries. Most towns had a workhouse, and records can be found in the County Records Office. Orphanages and homes for the infirm and disabled were another tangible and poignant product of the Victorian interest in charitable works. It is worth trying to find documentary material from such places as these can elicit powerful empathetic reactions from children. The work of the Salvation Army after 1878 is also important in the provision of shelter for the homeless.

William Booth (1829–1912) founded the Salvation Army, a Christian organisation against poverty. His inspiration came from his own faith and his dismay at the plight of the poor and outcast.

Charles Dickens (1812–1870) was a journalist and novelist. He was a social campaigner and many of his books reflect social injustices.

What you need and preparation

Collect information on local poor provision (for example workhouse, local asylums for physically disabled, charity schools, orphanages, soup kitchens or hostels for homeless). Prepare copies of photocopiable sheets 107 and 108 (one between two). Have available a copy of Charles Dickens' *A Christmas Carol* and/or *Oliver Twist*, local directories, scrap paper, writing materials and access to a board or flipchart. Check in advance for any cereal allergies, then just before the session, prepare some cold gruel (very weak water porridge, unsalted) and some stale hard wholemeal bread. Supply one spoon per child in the class. You will also need a video showing the workhouse scene from the film of *Oliver Twist*.

What to do

Introduction
5 mins Introduce the objective of lesson to look at the provision for the poor and helpless.

Development
80 mins Ask the children to work in small groups to list the sort of people who would fall into the category of poor according to Victorians. Ask for contributions, listing the types on the board. Make sure the list includes those who were disabled from birth or from injury, orphans, the sick, those out of work, the old and the homeless. Emphasise that there was no benefit system. If a family couldn't support those unable to work or if they had no family, then they were literally on the streets.

Read the extract from Charles Dickens' *A Christmas Carol* when Scrooge rebuffs the approach of the charity collectors for contributions to the orphan provision. Summarise the attitudes of self-help, laissez-faire and the deserving poor. Ask the children why Dickens wrote this. What was he trying to say? Was Scrooge's view normal or not? How could we find out? (Lead the children to suggest reference to other fiction works and the letters column in national newspapers of the time.)

What about practical help? If people held this view, would they contribute to charity provision? Make connections with modern charity provision and appeals. It is clear that whilst some of these attitudes persisted, especially the concept of the deserving poor, a considerable amount of energy was put into providing for the poor by individuals and charitable groups.

Spend some time talking about the work of William Booth and the Salvation Army, which involved

Learning objectives
● Be aware of what constituted the group called 'the poor'.
● Give examples of official and charitable provision for the poor, including faith-based provision, both nationally and locally.
● Understand the concepts of 'laissez-faire' and the 'deserving' and 'undeserving poor' and 'self-help'.

Lesson organisation
Whole class, with teacher-input; small group discussion, then teacher-input, class discussion work in pairs, class feedback and individual work; whole class.

Vocabulary
workhouse
Salvation Army
William Booth
deserving poor
laissez-faire
able-bodied
indigent
orphan
orphanage
asylum
Charles Dickens

providing hostel accommodation for the homeless as an extension of their Christian duty, and also preaching to them and converting them to Christianity as they went about it. This was only one example of religious involvement in charity provision for the poor. Virtually all religious groups supported some sort of charitable provision in the form of donations of money and goods (blankets, clothes, food, medicines).

Ask children to work in pairs to examine copies of local directory entries for clues about local poor provision and record their finds on paper. Invite pairs to feed back to the whole class, then talk about local examples of provision, for example orphanages, hostels, soup-kitchens, asylums for the sick or disabled. (As an alternative, you could create a worksheet on just one example of poor provision based on local sources.)

Describe the official government response to the problem of poverty, especially for the able-bodied out of work (1834 Poor Law Amendment Act). Summarise the prevailing theory of making the workhouse so unattractive that people would not want to go there, but would make greater effort to seek work. It certainly worked as a deterrent, as many preferred to face death and danger on the streets rather than give themselves over to the local workhouse.

Describe, preferably with illustrations from local examples, the organisation and activities of the workhouse, for example long hours of work doing unpaid work like oakum-picking or laundry work; very limited food; very little provision for the sick; early apprenticeship of children; confinement to the workhouse grounds; no freedom of movement; burial in a pauper's grave after death. To illustrate the point, read from the book or show a video clip from *Oliver Twist* where Oliver is in a workhouse. Serve some gruel and hard stale bread for the children to sample, and remind them that this was the usual staple diet for people living in a workhouse.

Using photocopiable pages 107 and 108 for reference (or your own material from a local workhouse), ask the children to write a story about a new orphan's arrival at the gates of the workhouse. Suggest that the child's parents have died from cholera and relatives are unable to take him or her in. Ask them to describe the first few days in the workhouse and how it felt. Was the child befriended or bullied by the other children? Did the child get into trouble there?

5 mins Plenary
Read some examples of the children's creative writing. Recap on some of the ways people could end up being poor in Victorian times and the differences between then and now.

Differentiation
Differentiation will mainly be by outcome in the writing and questioning work. The directory work could be undertaken in mixed-ability pairs.

Assessing learning outcomes
Can the children write a story including accurate references to conditions for children in a workhouse? Can they empathise with children in the workhouse? Can they extract information on local poor provision from directories? Can they understand that fiction is sometimes written with a particular motive in mind?

ICT opportunities
● Enter local workhouse or orphanage evidence into a database for ease of use.
● Let children word-process their stories.

Follow-up activity
Dramatise life in the workhouse or orphanage based on local primary evidence.

How did the Victorians deal with crime?

Background information

Law and order during the period showed a marked level of reform and saw the uniform provision of a country-wide police force. The Metropolitan Police Force was set up in London in 1829 by the then home secretary, Sir Robert Peel (from whom the police got the nicknames 'bobbies' and 'peelers'). By 1856 this police force was to be replicated by law in all counties. In 1853 transportation as a punishment was ended and in 1878 there was a commission set up to look into prison conditions. Prisoners were made to work in silence doing hard labour, such as picking oakum, on the treadmill or stone-breaking between the hours of 6am and 7pm. At other times they did purposeless work just to exhaust and break them, such as passing a heavy cannonball around a circle of prisoners continuously for hours, or walking on a wheel treadmill, or turning a crank.

Punishments for disobedience or misbehaviour in prison were severe, including being locked up in a dark cell alone for days and nights, a bread and water diet, having chains fastened to legs and wrists (irons), beating or flogging, and extra work. Cells were filthy and the food was seriously inadequate. Murderers were still hanged in public until 1868. Flogging and beating of prisoners was routine. Punishment for theft was severe and children were not exempt from the full rigour of the law.

In the second half of the period a change of attitude towards children led to the building of reform schools which were locked, residential houses of correction and training for child criminals. All the same, children of five and six years of age were placed in adult prisons as late as 1878 because of lack of space in the reform schools.

What you need and preparation

Prepare your own transcriptions or photocopies of local court records and newspaper reports on crime in Victorian times in your locality, one for each pair of children. Make copies of photocopiable pages 109 and 110 for each child. Have available a video of *Oliver Twist*, and illustrations of early Victorian policemen with uniform and equipment (whistle and truncheon). Prepare labels for the foundation of the police force, its nationwide extension, the repeal of public hanging, and the repeal of transportation for the class timeline.

**CHAPTER 1
THE VICTORIANS**

Victorian
towns and
town life

What to do

(10 mins) Introduction
Show the extract of *Oliver Twist* where Oliver is caught for theft and brought up before the magistrate. Discuss with the children the problems of crime in towns, particularly theft (links to poverty) and violence.

(75 mins) Development
Talk about law enforcement prior to Robert Peel's innovations, for example the parish constable and night watch, then magistrates. Describe the creation of the police service and talk about the origins of the nicknames 'bobbies' and 'peelers'. Display pictures of policemen of the time, and talk about their uniform and equipment, and how the police force was all male. Talk about its spread by law to all counties by 1860.

Using the photocopiable source extracts on page 109, summarise the prevalence of crime and the sentences that those crimes merited, especially against the young. Describe prison conditions, which included hard labour, flogging and other punishments, and poor food. Ask the children to form groups of up to six to discuss the deterrent power of these sentences. Would they restrict crime or not? Stress that the groups must be able to justify their reasoning. Then invite the groups to feed back their conclusions to the whole class. Stress the significance of necessity as an issue in crime against property and desperation leading to violence where hanging was the penalty.

Give out photocopies or transcriptions of local magistrates or county court records for the period listing crimes and sentences to mixed-ability pairs to read. Then ask them to work individually on photocopiable sheet 110 to write their own fictional newspaper account of a local crime, and the subsequent trial and sentence of the criminal.

(5 mins) Plenary
Place the law and order reforms on the class timeline. Ask the children to tell you where to place the labels for the foundation of the police force, its nationwide extension, the repeal of public hanging, and the repeal of transportation.

Differentiation
Make a simple comprehension worksheet to accompany photocopiable page 109 for poorer readers and writers.

Assessing learning outcomes
Can the children recall the key events in law and order reforms during the period? Can they discuss the impact of severe penalties on criminal activity and present logical arguments for their views showing awareness of the real situation? Can the children use primary sources to produce a likely scenario of a crime and trial in a newspaper format?

ICT opportunities
• The children could make a newspaper page on the computer.
• Court records could be transcribed on to a database.

Follow-up activities
• Contact the local police station and ask about its history.
• Analyse local court records for evidence of the type and frequency of crimes and sentences handed out, together with the age and sex of the criminal.

34

PRIMARY FOUNDATIONS: *History Ages 9–11*

Britain since 1930

This National Curriculum History study unit has two main choices in its content. The first is an in-depth focus study of the impact of the World War II on the lives of men, women and children, with particular reference to the situation in Britain, rather than a history of military events. The second is a longitudinal study charting change through the decades from 1930 onwards, with specific reference to technological and social change. This unit, perhaps better than any other, gives children the opportunity to compare several different periods of time. It also lends itself to independent research-based historical enquiry.

Both themes have a great deal of potential to offer Key Stage 2 children. Easily accessible sources of evidence are plentiful, including oral evidence and film archive material. The variety and contrasts in evidence also allow children to understand the subtleties of bias and the uniqueness of individual experience. The content also permits exploration of political history, particularly war and its impact on daily life, propaganda and changes in social values. There is much potential for the delivery of PSHE with issues of gender and race discrimination, drugs and sex education, social responsibility, the spirit of community and the fight for liberty and democracy.

The years of the 20th century have involved rapid change and global conflict. Within the span of just one generation alone lifestyles, attitudes and opportunities can differ dramatically. Teachers in their mid-twenties can find themselves genuinely saying that 'it wasn't like that in my day!'

In 1930, Britain was about to plunge into a period of economic depression, mass unemployment and deep poverty caused by the collapse of the American Stock Exchange in 1929 (the Wall Street Crash). No sooner had the country climbed precariously out of depression than Germany's expansionist policies led to World War II. That war, like the one previously, was to have a lasting effect on Britain and its people. The recent sixtieth anniversaries of the Dunkirk evacuation and the Battle of Britain revived powerful emotions and exposed deeply-embedded memories of life and events then.

The post-war period saw a time of readjustment, particularly for women, as men demobilised from the war. Despite the continuing rationing and austerity, ideological ideas germinating in the crisis years of the war led to the creation in 1948 of the Health Service and Social Security systems, the provision of universal secondary education for children to the age of 15 and the universal National Insurance and Pension Scheme to provide for sickness, unemployment and old age. It was a period of genuine political idealism.

Technological and medical advances continued apace, particularly in the fields of entertainment, communication, computer technology, transport (including space travel), medicine and warfare. In almost every field there was a corresponding impact on daily life, drawn against a background of international political dangers and developments, the Cold War, the Cuban Crisis, the EEC, the United Nations, the Civil Rights Movement and the anti-nuclear campaign, led by CND.

Britain since 1930 is a study rich in interest and relevance and is well worth exploring.

What was life like in Britain during World War II?

World War II was one of the first wars to result in massive civilian deaths, a feature of later 20th century wars. Those six years of war between 1939 and 1945 saw the mass evacuation of children from their city homes and families, rationing, public propaganda campaigns, the blackout, the Blitz and, for the second time that century, the involvement of women in every conceivable 'male' job except front-line combat. It also involved the commitment of the whole Commonwealth, with troops from India, Africa, Australasia and the West Indies fighting for Britain.

Against this background, ordinary lives continued. Simultaneously with the evacuation of children on the day war was declared, all men between the ages of 18 and 41 were called up into the services and reported for action. Rationing was introduced, especially on petrol and food. Identity cards had to be carried at all times, along with gas masks. Posters and radio programmes urged the population to 'keep mum' and to be aware that 'walls have ears'. Fear of fifth columnists (spies) getting information and infiltrating was rife. More prosaic propaganda persuaded people to 'make do and mend' or 'dig for victory', both ways of ameliorating the effects of food, clothing and materials shortages. Censorship in the press and the use of war films to keep up spirits and stiffen resolve are fruitful areas for exploration with the children.

Most adults had two jobs during the war, their paid work and then their voluntary war work in the evenings and at weekends or when not on shift. Families and communities stuck together and although the 'business as usual' spirit was utilised effectively as a political morale-boosting tool, it was nevertheless a reality in many communities. There was a powerful determination to resist, although recent revisionist works based on the Mass Observation unit research have challenged this view.

The war was a period of extreme crisis, underpinned by stringent regulations and hardship. It is a period of history that still provokes emotional responses in children, let alone participants. Care must be taken in this study not to unintentionally glorify war or stereotype experiences. Anti-German feeling can arise and at its worst children can see war as an exciting, ennobling, bloodthirsty adventure. At the same time sensitive children can be distressed by graphic descriptions of the Blitz and the pain of separation experienced by many children when parted from their families. Sensitivity is also needed by children when asking for personal recollections from those involved. Nevertheless the event is important. It still influences current affairs and is part of our national history.

UNIT: What was life like in Britain during World War II?

Enquiry questions	Learning objectives	Teaching activities	Learning outcomes	Literacy links	Cross-curricular links
What was World War II?	• Know when World War II happened. • Know who was involved. • Understand in simple terms the reasons for the war. • Know who Winston Churchill was and what his role was. • Know the key events of the war affecting the population of Britain. • Imagine what it was like to be a child on the day war broke out.	Teacher input on causes, combatants and dates of the war. Listen to Winston Churchill's speeches and watch film clips. Describe the key events in the passage of the war, for example Dunkirk, Battle of Britain, Blitz, D-Day landings and VE Day. Comprehension exercise on information including timeline activity recording key dates. Using film clip of war declaration, explore the feelings of a family at that moment. Dramatise scenes of family using broadcast as stimulus or creative writing. Gather evidence from families and also artefacts concerning the war. Read part of fiction story set in World War II	Children: • recount the circumstances of the war, including dates, key events in Britain and the key British leader • imagine what it was like to be a child at the moment war broke out • understand that during World War II Britain faced invasion and occupation	Fiction texts exploring the war or *War Boy* by Michael Foreman as an autobiography; different genres and emotive language; comprehension skills.	PSHE: empathise with people in crisis and to express in words and actions how they might have felt; understand that at times it is necessary to fight to retain democratic freedoms.
What was it like to be evacuated?	• Know the reasons for the evacuation of children from cities. • Make deductions from eye-witness accounts about what it was like to be evacuated. • Imagine what it was like to be evacuated.	Extract from fiction set in period. Brief input on evacuation, reasons, procedures and outcomes. Use evidence showing a range of experiences. Exploration of arguments for and against evacuation. Vote on whether they would allow their children to be evacuated. Write a letter to an evacuated child, or write as an evacuated child describing experiences and feelings.	• explain what evacuation was for and who was affected by it • justify a particular point of view concerning evacuation • are aware that there was a range of views concerning evacuation • write imaginatively about evacuation	Writing in different forms; explanatory text and exposition.	
What was the Blitz?	• Know what is meant by the Blitz. • Know why it happened. • Know the impact of the Blitz on the locality. • Imagine what it was like to be in a city being blitzed. • Know about the role of the civil defence groups.	Input on Battle of Britain and then Blitz, using TV film archive and sound effects, including the reasons for the attack on civilian communities. Examine the effect of the Blitz on the nearest city. Look at defence against Blitz – air raid shelters, air raid sirens, anti-aircraft guns, barrage balloons, blackout, gas masks. Examine impact on communities not experiencing direct attack, for example rural communities. Research roles of civil defence groups. Dramatise air raid.	• understand the impact of the Blitz on local and city communities • appreciate that not everyone was blitzed • are aware of the specific roles of key workers helping during the Blitz • re-enact a scene of an air raid		Art/design and technology: construct pâpier maché helmets for workers; construct an Anderson shelter from corrugated cardboard.
What was rationing?	• Understand the reason for rationing. • Know what rationing meant in real terms to the lives of individuals. • Know some of the other ways the Government promoted the conservation of resources.	Input on the need to conserve resources (imports being attacked). Describe and demonstrate coupons. Show weekly rations in food terms including free produce. Show posters, dig for victory, pig bins, metal collections, and 'thrifty recipes'. Make a carrot cake and have a 'war time tea'. Discuss the 'black market' and its operation.	• appreciate the need for conserving resources • know the ways conservation was practised during the war • know how difficult it was to manage on rationed clothing, petrol and food • are aware of the existence of a black market in rationed goods	Awareness of persuasive language used to alter behaviours.	Design and technology: cooking following a recipe. Maths: using weights and measures accurately.
Why were propaganda and censorship employed during the war?	• Know what propaganda and censorship are. • Understand why these were employed.	Input on definition of propaganda. Examination of examples of propaganda posters and censorship techniques. Identify use of persuasive and emotive language. Consider the morality of these techniques.	• know about the persuasive and manipulative messages given by the government during the war. • know that information about the progress of the war was censored.	Use of persuasive and effective language.	Citizenship: awareness of the dangers of censorship and propaganda.
What was it like on VE Day?	• Know when VE Day was and what it celebrated. • Empathise with people at the time.	Input on VE Day and VJ Day. Discussion on what it would have felt like on VE Day, using film archive material, newspapers and so on. Examination of the problems facing Britain in the aftermath of war.	• know what VE Day was • know how it was celebrated • recognise that the end of the war brought problems as well as relief and joy.		PSHE: empathy. Citizenship: the need for peace.

What was life like in Britain during World War II?

1 hour What was World War II?

Learning objectives
• Know when World War II happened and who was involved.
• Understand in simple terms the reasons for it.
• Know who Winston Churchill was and what his role was in the war.
• Know the key events of the war affecting the population of Britain.

Lesson organisation
Teacher-led input to whole class; individual work on comprehension; whole class, teacher-led summary.

Vocabulary
World War II
Hitler
Fascism
Churchill
Allies
British
Expeditionary
Force
troops
Dunkirk
Battle of Britain
Blitz
Pearl Harbor
D-Day
VE and VJ Day

Background information

World War II happened between the years 1939 and 1945 as a result of the rise of fascism and the expansionist policies of Germany, but also involved the other axis powers, Italy and Japan. Initially Stalinist Russia aligned itself with Germany but switched sides and was subsequently attacked by Germany. The Allied powers included France, Britain and from December 1941, America.

Following Germany's invasion of Poland in September 1939, Britain's overseas involvement in the war was immediate and unsuccessful. By June 1940 Britain was the only Allied power not occupied by German or Italian troops. The evacuation of British troops from Dunkirk by the 'little boats' in the face of heavy German assault was both a critical low point and a rallying cry for determined resistance. What followed was a period of attrition and destruction, endured and survived by the population of Britain and led indomitably by the coalition leader Winston Churchill.

The RAF Battle of Britain, an air battle, only just kept the Germans from invading in September 1940. At that time the Blitz began with the systematic bombing of military, service and civilian targets in Britain, designed to destroy the military, communications and economic infrastructure of the country and lower morale with the intention of making invasion and occupation easier.

This 'back to the wall' defence continued until USA entered the war on the Allied side following the Japanese bombing of Pearl Harbor. With the additional resources of the Americans and the disastrous campaigns on the Russian Front by Hitler, the Allies were able to plan a military offensive. Italy capitulated in 1943 in the face of invasion. The D-Day landings of 1944 marked a direct assault on German troops and on 7 May 1945 Germany surrendered (VE Day was 8 May). The dropping of the atom bombs on Japan that year marked the end of the war in the Far East (14 August 1945; VJ Day was 2 September 1945) and the return of many of the British prisoners-of-war held in Japanese camps.

What you need and preparation

Obtain video footage of events during the war, plus tape recordings of Neville Chamberlain and Winston Churchill's speeches, and replica newspapers from the era. Prepare individual copies of photocopiable pages 111 and 112. Prepare a class timeline from 1930 to 1950 and make labels for the Declaration of War, Dunkirk, Battle of Britain, Blitz, US entry into the war, D-Day, VE Day and VJ Day. You will need access to a board or flipchart, a cassette player and a video.

What to do

5 mins Introduction
Ask the children what they know about World War II. Record any correct facts on the board.

45 mins Development
Talk about the key dates, causes and progress of the war, keeping things basic. Cover the Declaration (3 September 1939), Dunkirk (June 1940), Battle of Britain (September 1940), the Blitz (September 1940 onwards), the Bombing of Pearl Harbor and the American entry into the war (December 1941), the D-Day landings (June 1944), VE Day (8 May 1945), VJ Day (2 September 1945). Use film archive material and newspapers to illustrate the events. Include reference to Winston Churchill and his role as Prime Minister. Play a recording of one of his inspirational speeches, for example 'We will fight them on the beaches' (following Dunkirk), together with the recording of Chamberlain's announcement that Britain was now at war with Germany.

Then let the children complete the worksheet on photocopiable page 111 and plot the events in the correct place on the timeline on photocopiable page 112.

CHAPTER 2
BRITAIN SINCE 1930

What was life
like in Britain
during World
War II?

Plenary
10 mins Have a question-and-answer session to place key events on the class timeline, based on the children's responses to photocopiable page 111.

Differentiation
The worksheet has graded questions getting more challenging as they progress. Support children of lower ability by making a simpler version of the task sheet, with answers provided from which to choose.

Assessing learning outcomes
Do the children know when World War II was, why it was fought and the key events affecting the British? Are they able to name the wartime Prime Minister and give reasons for his fame? Can they record the key events of the war on an individual timeline?

ICT opportunities
Children could prepare and print off a family questionnaire about wartime experiences.

Follow-up activities
● Have a drama session focusing on the immediate feelings of a family at the moment war was declared, using the broadcast by Chamberlain as a stimulus.
● Let children conduct a survey among older family members about their recollections or experiences of World War II.
● In PSHE, have a discussion on the nature of war and its dilemmas.
● Read fiction set in World War II, for example Michelle Magorian's *Goodnight Mr Tom* or Robert Westall's *Machine-Gunners*.

What was it like to be evacuated?
1 hour

Background information
Following the invasion of Poland on 1 September 1939, a massive planned evacuation programme of children from British cities to the countryside was instituted by the government to keep them safe from bombing. 1.2 million children were moved between 1 and 4 September. It was expected that from the day war was declared German bombers would be flying overhead dropping bombs and poison gas, hence the universal distribution of gas masks. Unfortunately, because the bombing didn't materialise in the 'Phoney War' period of 1939 and 40, many children returned to the cities only to die in the subsequent Blitz. Poison gas was never used, however.

Evacuation meant that thousands of children left the only home and community they knew for strange places, people and lifestyles. Their fortunes were mixed. Some recount that they had a wonderful time; others tell of strong and persistent feelings of loneliness and fear, confusion and intimidation. Experiences of mistreatment, of being used as unpaid labour, and of abuse are frequent. Billeting was compulsory, so it is not surprising that experiences were mixed. Returning home presented further problems of adjustment. Homes and streets were sometimes gone completely. Families were damaged and decimated, yet lives had to go on. Evacuation left powerful memories.

What you need and preparation
Collect extracts of evacuation eye-witness accounts from family surveys done by the children themselves and photographs of evacuees from information books. Prepare copies of photocopiable page 113 for each child. Have available a video and video footage of evacuation, a recording of the opening scene of *Goodnight Mr Tom* or the opening chapter of *Carrie's War* by Nina Bawden.

What to do
Introduction
10 mins Recap on the beginning of World War II and the evacuation of children from the cities. Read the opening of *Carrie's War*, or show the opening sequence of *Goodnight Mr Tom*, or video extracts of evacuation footage. Discuss the reasons for evacuation and the procedures (for example labelling the children, not knowing the destination, travelling in groups into the countryside, being billeted to communities and households sometimes against the will or desire of the owners).

Ask how we could find out more about what it was like to be evacuated (by reading accounts or talking to people who were evacuated as children).

Learning objectives
● Know what evacuation of children was during the war.
● Understand the reasons for evacuation.
● Appreciate that there were different views about the rightness of evacuation.
● Be able to empathise with parents faced with the evacuation of their children.

Lesson organisation
Whole class with teacher input; mixed-ability pairs then individual feedback to whole class, with discussion in small groups; individual voting.

Vocabulary
evacuation
Blitz
billet
billeting officer

What was life like in Britain during World War II?

Follow-up activities
• Make evacuation labels and gas mask boxes in technology.
• Role play evacuation – parting with parents, travelling for the first time, waiting in a village hall to be chosen by foster parents, settling in.
• Write letters, either as an evacuated child telling of their experiences or as a parent explaining why the child cannot come home yet.
• Discuss parental responsibilities and the dilemmas that faced World War II parents.

Development
45 mins Let children work in mixed-ability pairs to examine the extracts on photocopiable page 113, plus any other eye-witness accounts you have available, to find out what evacuation was like.

Invite children to feed back to the rest of the class the range of experiences of the evacuees, both the bad things and the good.

The class can then discuss in small groups the arguments for and against evacuation, considering the situation then. Ask them to write down their arguments for feedback to the whole class.

Plenary
5 mins Ask the children to imagine that they are parents and that there is a war on. Evacuation is ordered from the towns and cities. Would they send their children away or not? Take a vote then ask for justifications for individual decisions.

Differentiation
Use mixed-ability grouping and pairing for source work and discussion. Less confident readers could be placed with more confident readers. Support discussion if necessary.

Assessing learning outcomes
Can the children use documentary sources to find out what it was like to be evacuated? Can they recognise that experiences could be both good and bad and analyse arguments for and against evacuation? Can they justify a decision to evacuate or not based on rational and empathetic thought?

1 hour — What was the Blitz?

Learning objectives
• Know what the Blitz was and its effect on communities.
• Know what defence measures were used to help protect from the effect of bombing.
• Know about the role of volunteers in civil defence.

Lesson organisation
Whole class, with teacher-led input; groups of three for research work; individual presentations to whole class.

Background information
The Blitz made a major impact on life in the cities. There was widespread destruction and death, often concentrated in intense periods of night and daylight bombing. It was profoundly shocking for those involved, bringing desperate and continuous fear of death and dislocation, poverty and insecurity. It created millions of refugees, homeless, possessionless and traumatised.

Public air raid shelters had already been hastily constructed to take civilian occupants. Some households had bought their own Anderson shelter to dig into the garden. Others relied on the Morrison indoor shelter. Air raid sirens blared out the warning wail and the all-clears, and the civil defence units were constituted and went about their work, including the Home Guard, the air raid wardens, the fire fighters and later the heavy rescue squads and ambulance drivers. The blackout was introduced to prevent enemy bombers getting fixes on civilian targets, a precaution that in its initial stringency caused more deaths through accidents than it prevented through bombing.

What you need and preparation
Collect together photographs and, if possible, film footage of the Blitz, plus sound effects (for example, BBC Radio sound effects cassette), together with a video and a cassette player. Find as many secondary information books and CD-ROMs on the subject as possible. Provide writing paper (for both rough and final work), pens, felt-tipped pens and crayons.

What to do
Introduction
10 mins Show the film footage of the Blitz or play the sound effects tape, and talk about the Blitz, why it happened and what it involved. Show the children photographs of the bomb damage. Talk about what it must have been like to live through the Blitz.

CHAPTER 2
BRITAIN SINCE 1930

What was life
like in Britain
during World
War II?

(40 mins) Development

Ask the children to work in threes to find out about one sort of defence and/or type of volunteer job using information books and CD-ROMs. Allocate topics from the following list: air raid shelters, blackout, anti-aircraft guns, barrage balloons, gas masks (for adults, children and babies), air raid sirens, air raid wardens, fire crews, bomb disposal units, heavy rescue squads, ambulance drivers, home guard, WRVS (Women's Royal Voluntary Service) and Red Cross.

Ask the children to make notes on rough paper at first, then to present their work neatly with illustrations for display.

Ask the groups to prepare a brief presentation to the rest of class about their findings.

(10 mins) Plenary

Allow each group a minute for their presentations.

Conclude the lesson with a mock air raid alert, with the children taking shelter under the desks. Stress that the children need to stay there until the all-clear sounds.

Differentiation

Use mixed-ability groups to allow children to support each other. Allow for differentiation of tasks within the groups, including provision of illustrations, writing up and oral presentation.

Assessing learning outcomes

Can the children use secondary information books to find out about an aspect of the Blitz? Can they summarise information in visual, written and oral forms?

Vocabulary
Blitz
bombing
incendiaries
doodle-bugs
air raid wardens
fire crews
heavy rescue
squads
bomb disposal units
blackout
Anderson shelter
Morrison shelter
air raid shelter
air raid siren
anti-aircraft guns
flack
barrage balloons
gas masks

ICT opportunities
Record specific raids on a database, charting date, time, location (street), types of bomb, and damage in terms of deaths, injuries and destruction of buildings. Use air raid wardens' logs from your local public record office for information. Analyse the evidence for intensity of raids, casualties in weekly or daily totals, and types of weapon. Use the word processor to write up the information found for display.

Follow-up activities
● Research into eye-witness accounts of the Blitz, identifying what it was like to be in the Blitz. Use this for drama work portraying the fear of the situation, the danger and the work of the rescue squads. Use recorded sound effects to aid empathy.
● Use local newspaper accounts to examine the impact of the Blitz on your nearest city, but also the absence of Blitz experiences for those living in the countryside. Compare the front pages of a local rural and a city newspaper from your local history library or public records office.
● Make helmets as used by various volunteer forces, with their designated initials, such as ARP (Air Raid Precaution), AFS (Auxiliary Fire Service), FC (Fire Crew), HR (Heavy Rescue), etc.
● Research into wartime work – Women's Land Army, WRVS, transport, munitions, medicine and nursing, factory work, auxiliary work (at army bases, military land convoys, etc), especially the role of women.
● Using log books, photos and eye-witness accounts, look at schooling during the Blitz.

CHAPTER 2
BRITAIN SINCE 1930

What was life like in Britain during World War II?

1 hour What was rationing?

Learning objectives
• Understand the need for rationing during the war.
• Know what rationing meant to the lives of individuals.
• Know some of the other ways the Government encouraged the conservation of resources.

Lesson organisation
Whole class, with teacher-led input; whole class then mixed-ability pairs or threes; whole class, with teacher-led recap and individual children illustrating points.

Vocabulary
rationing
coupons
utility
austerity
black market
resources

Background information
As an island nation, Britain needed to import goods to function. During the war, merchant shipping was attacked and sunk. Supplies became very scarce, including foodstuffs and petrol and raw materials such as iron and cotton.

Rationing was therefore phased in as follows: January 1940 food rationed; March 1940 meat, clothes and coal rationed; March 1942 white bread banned (flour shortage), utility clothes introduced; July 1942 sweets rationed; October 1942 milk ration cut.

What you need and preparation
Buy in advance a week's food ration, based on the information on photocopiable page 114. Have available secondary information texts and CD-ROMs covering aspects of rationing, utility and propaganda posters, a video and a video recording of an episode of *Dad's Army* that shows Private Walker dealing in black market goods. Prepare copies of photocopiable pages 114 and 115 (one between two). Provide writing and drawing equipment for making propaganda posters. Write on the board the following key words: 'Problem: Resource shortage. Solution?'

What to do

10 mins ### Introduction
Talk about the reasons why Britain had to conserve its resources. Ask the children what they would have done if they had been in charge of the country in this situation.

Briefly discuss strategies for conservation of resources, using the key words written on the board. Group the children's responses around five essential ideas – restricting consumption, encouraging thrifty attitudes, recycling, maximising home produce, protecting imports.

40 mins ### Development
Talk about rationing and how it was phased in. Use the information on photocopiable page 114 to show the coupon and points system and the weekly ration of basic foodstuffs. Display the real goods to show what this meant. Point out that there were no chocolates or sweets. Stress that having lots of money wouldn't have helped you to get more; rich or poor, you could only have that much. Use the eye-witness accounts on photocopiable page 115 to illustrate the problems associated with rationing.

Split the class up into pairs or threes, and let them have copies of the photocopiable pages for reference. Then ask them to use secondary information books and primary sources to find out about different methods of conserving resources. Explain that each group is to produce an example of the method, for example a poster or slogan, a recipe or a demonstration to encourage or inform. Allocate the tasks as follows:
• examples of encouraging thrift, for example recipes, tips for recycling such as making over clothing, demonstrations
• public information posters and slogans (Make do and mend, dig for victory, is your journey really necessary?), also public advice about nutrition
• public collections of iron (salvage), food waste for the pigs (pig bins), cultivation of common land or public areas for food production
• utility clothing and furniture – what were they and what were they like?
• home-grown and reared food (free from rationing), for example rearing hens for eggs and meat, growing your own vegetables and keeping a cow or goat for free milk (unpasteurised).

10 mins Plenary
Recap on the methods used to overcome the problem of conservation of resources. Invite the children to illustrate the various methods they have researched. Introduce the idea of the black market, and show the extract from *Dad's Army*. Ask the children about the morality of this. Would they buy on the black market?

Differentiation
Mixed-ability pairs or threes could be used to support children of lower ability. Offer support with secondary information books for children of lower ability.

Assessing learning outcomes
Can they use primary and secondary sources of information to find out about methods of coping with shortages? Can they consider the moral issues of dealing on the black market and justify their reasoning?

1 hour Why were propaganda and censorship employed during the war?

Background information
During the war, propaganda techniques included posters and slogans, public broadcasts on radio and in the press and films, and manipulation of the news to play up victories and play down setbacks. Many posters were produced with slogans such as 'Kill Him with War Savings' (encouraging investment in savings bonds to fund the war effort). Hitler was frequently portrayed as an insect or a devil. By contrast, Winston Churchill and the Allied forces were consistently shown as heroic, as in the Battle of Britain poster which showed the words 'Never was so much owed by so many to so few' spoken by the Prime Minister, with a picture of an air crew underneath.

Censorship was also a prominent feature of wartime life. Its aim was to keep information of strategic importance from the enemy at the same time as keeping morale and confidence up amongst the nation. Methods included the vetting of all newspapers, radio broadcasts and films, and the actual filtering of information given to the press and radio by suppressing or distorting the truth such as numbers of British planes shot down or deaths in air raids. Successful allied action was played up and exaggerated. Tone of delivery, music or vocabulary were also used to manipulate the emotions of the nation.

What you need and preparation
Obtain examples of propaganda posters (The Imperial War Museum is a good source) and national or local newspaper headlines about the Battle of Britain or the Blitz. If possible, obtain a recording of a government-sponsored feature film of the time, such as *In Which We Serve*, *The Gentler Sex* or *Mrs Miniver*, and a video. Prepare copies of photocopiable pages 116 and 117. Make sure the children have writing materials, and that you have access to a flipchart or board.

What to do
5 mins Introduction
Explain that this lesson will look at two important aspects of wartime, censorship and propaganda. Ask the children for a definition of propaganda. Record their ideas on the board around the key word propaganda. Help them to a basic definition (for example organised attempts to put forward a particular idea or view to make people believe and think and act in a certain way). Point out that advertisements could be described as commercial propaganda.

What was life like in Britain during World War II?

ICT opportunities
Identify the powerful use of film and radio media to influence national morale. Link with the use of media today.

Follow-up activities
• Discuss issues of citizenship and the voluntary suspension of freedom of information, including the dangers (for example Hitler's Fascism, the Stalinist re-writing of history).
• Invite two guest speakers to talk about wartime childhood experiences, preferably giving different views. Children should prepare questions and record in report form what was found out through this oral evidence.
• Listen to and learn World War II songs that have an emotive content ('The White Cliffs of Dover', 'We'll Meet Again', etc).

Development
45 mins The children will already be familiar with examples of propaganda from work on evacuation and rationing. Show a selection of examples of propaganda posters. Ask the children what message these were supposed to deliver. How do they play on people's emotions? Look at extract from a government-sponsored film such as *In Which We Serve*, *The Gentler Sex* or *Mrs Miniver*. Ask the children to identify emotive filming techniques (dialogue, plot and music).

Give out copies of photocopiable page 116, one between two, to half the class. This requires the children to record their answers on paper or in an exercise book. Give the other half of the class copies of photocopiable page 117, which looks at censorship. Ask them to work in pairs on the questions about the extract (from the *Daily Telegraph* of 15 July 1940, following the Dunkirk evacuation). Remind them about Dunkirk if necessary.

Alternatively, you could use a local newspaper account of Blitz raids. Ask the children to examine what is said and what is deliberately omitted. Identify any emotive words and morale-boosting phrases. Ask them to look out for adjacent reports that tell of British gains or successes. How would it have made them feel if they had read this page in their newspaper?

Plenary
10 mins Invite representatives from the two groups to feed back information to the whole class. Discuss the problem of censorship and propaganda. Is it right and justifiable for an elected democratic government to permit distortion of the truth or even blatant lying? Reiterate the reasons for it, but allow the children to hold independent views.

Differentiation
Pupils of lower ability should work orally on photocopiable page 116 only with the teacher in a small group, answering the worksheet questions before recording their answers.

Other children can work on photocopiable page 117 in mixed-ability pairs.

Assessing learning outcomes
Can the children recognise the elements used in propaganda and censorship? Do they know why these techniques were used? Can the children rationally discuss the morality of these techniques in a democratic society?

1 hour What was it like on VE Day?

Background information
VE Day (Victory in Europe Day) happened on Tuesday 8 May 1945, and marked the end of the war throughout Europe. The war continued in the Far East ending on VJ Day on 2 September that year, but for the people of Britain celebrations began for real in May.

Each town arranged its own formal celebrations. Church Services of Thanksgiving were held on the day itself. Bells were rung for the first time since the war began. (Bell-ringing had been banned during the war except as an alert to German invasion, so to hear the peel of bells without fear meant a great deal to the people.) Similarly the towns and cities were lit up as much as possible. Firework displays were arranged and bonfires lit, with an overall rejoicing at the removal of the blackout restrictions and the corresponding fear of bombing.

Many informal celebrations started on Monday night and continued all through the day and

evening of Tuesday. There were street parties in practically every street. In cities, people congregated in squares and public parks, dancing, drinking and singing. In London, thousands gathered in Trafalgar Square, Piccadilly Circus, the Mall and outside the Palace for the Royal appearance on the balcony. The mood was reported to have been one of pure frenzied joy and relief. Peace had come at last.

What you need and preparation
Obtain film archive footage of VE Day, plus a video, and photographs of the celebrations. Prepare VE and VJ Day labels for the class timeline. Prepare copies of photocopiable pages 118 and 119, one per child. Provide writing equipment. You will need access to a board or flipchart.

What to do

(5 mins) Introduction
Talk about the conclusion of the war, giving the two key dates – 8 May 1945 VE Day (Victory in Europe) and 2 September 1945 VJ Day (Victory in Japan). Place these two events on the class timeline.

(50 mins) Development
Ask the children to imagine what it would have felt like on the day Germany surrendered. What would they have done? Show some film archive footage and photographs of the VE Day celebrations.

Give out copies of photocopiable page 118 and ask the children to work in threes to identify key words to reflect the feelings expressed. Then ask them to record these words on photocopiable page 119 around the words 'The war is over!' Encourage feedback to the whole class. Record their chosen words on board.

Ask the children to work in small groups and pretend they are government ministers. Ask them to identify and discuss the problems that faced the nation after the celebrations ended. Ask each group to focus on one of five areas:
- the destruction of cities and towns from bomb damage
- the return home of people on active service
- the return of evacuees to their families
- the spending of all the nation's money on fighting the war
- the freeing of Italian and German prisoners of war.

Tell the groups that their task is to come up with a programme of action to solve these problems.

Allow feedback, problem by problem, to the whole class. Explain what did happen after the war.

(5 mins) Plenary
Put the key dates of the war on the board. Invite individual children to sum up what it was like during the war, and note down their key words on the board. Finish by rubbing off the words and replacing them with the word 'peace'. Remind the children that peace is by far a preferable state.

Differentiation
Less able children could look only at the visual material and then fill in their responses on photocopiable page 119. Mixed-ability pairs and groups could be used for the tasks.

Assessing learning outcomes
Can the children empathise with people on VE Day? Do they understand in basic terms the kinds of problems facing the nation following the end of the war?

Learning objectives
- Know what VE and VJ Day were.
- Know what it was like on the day the war ended.
- Empathise with people of the time.
- Know how people celebrated the end of the war.
- Understand some of the problems facing the country at the end of the war.

Lesson organisation
Whole class, with teacher-led input; mixed-ability threes, with one spokesperson to feed back to whole class; whole class, with teacher-led questioning.

Vocabulary
VE Day
VJ Day
victory
surrender
street party

Follow-up activities
- Discuss the value of peace and the role of the United Nations.
- Role-play a victory celebration street party in costume with food and songs.

How has life changed since 1930?

The principal historical concept developed through this theme is that of change. The evidence for this topic is rich and varied; indeed there is so much that selection becomes a problem. The same is true of the content of this topic. There is too much to cover.

Several approaches can be taken. A regional focus works well, charting change locally in streets, shops, schools and entertainment, and viewing national events through local people's experiences. Sources for this type of study include directories, OS maps, photos, film archives, newspapers and oral evidence. Alternatively lessons could be given on key types of change – social, technological, political, scientific, spiritual and environmental, for example. Another approach would be to select one of these themes and work through it decade by decade. Social history provides the most interesting base for this since it is about everyday life and attitudes.

This unit presents a different model, one that asks the children to act as independent researchers, consolidating their historical enquiry skills into a focused thematic study. The information will then be presented and shared and the issue of continuity considered. For this reason, the activities in this unit do not contain individual background information, but an overview of the period is given below.

Background information

The 1930s
Following the Wall Street collapse (1929), the early thirties were marked by extreme financial hardship for many people. It was a time of great poverty and unemployment. The Jarrow Hunger March to London took place in 1936. It highlighted the plight of the unemployed. Apart from a few workers covered by employment insurance schemes, people in hardship had to go to charitable aid or means-tested benefit for help.

Medical consultation and treatment had to be paid for. In consequence many illnesses went untreated, especially amongst women, as priority for medical treatment in the family would usually go to the breadwinner or to the children.

Cinema became a cheap and extremely popular form of mass entertainment. Films reflected the general need for escapism. Television was beginning to be available but for most people radio and newspapers were the main media of the day.

The jet engine was invented in 1930, marking the beginning of a new phase in air transport.

It was a time of political appeasement; but it was also the time of Mosley's blackshirts, whose aim was to bring about a fascist state in Britain. The threat of another world war, only a couple of decades after the previous one, was looming large throughout the period. It cast a shadow of fear across the country. The struggle to avoid war ended in 1939 when Britain took arms against the fascist axis powers of Germany and Italy.

The 1940s
This decade was dominated by the war and its aftermath. Rationing and austerity measures continued through the post-war reconstruction phase. It also saw the foundation of the welfare state, the NHS and social security systems and universal secondary education with its tripartite system of selection at 11 years of age (grammar, secondary modern and technical schools) based on newly-devised IQ tests. Penicillin was mass-produced as an antibiotic from 1947.

The 1950s
This decade saw a climbing out of the austerity of the post-war years. The Festival of Britain happened in 1951 as a celebration of the future. The coronation of Elizabeth II took place in 1953. In fashion, freedom from rationing was celebrated with wide skirts, and lots of petticoats. Rock and roll began to penetrate from America.

The structure of DNA was discovered by Watson and Crick, a prelude to gene technology. The polio vaccine (1956) made a major impact on child health.

Against the growing anxiety of the Cold War, Russia was sending satellites, then animals and eventually men into space. The UK was involved in the Korean War (1950–53). National Service was compulsory for all young men. There were labour shortages in many of the basic manual fields. Many Commonwealth citizens were invited to come to Britain to work.

The 1960s

Known as a decade of revolution, this packed ten years saw the rise of youth culture, of the peace movement and flower power, and of sexual freedom, aided by a booming economy permitting young people to leave home and work elsewhere. Jobs were plentiful and the mood was heady. Music broke away from previous conventions and became varied and innovative, for example the Beatles, Rolling Stones, etc. Recreational drug-taking and promiscuity became quite common amongst the young. Television became increasingly popular, especially with the introduction of colour in 1967.

The sixties was a time of anti-authoritarian, anti-establishment fever. The CND movement campaigned against nuclear weapons, its protests all the more urgent when the Cuban Crisis heightened fears of a nuclear holocaust. In America the civil rights movement went from strength to strength led by Martin Luther King. His campaign impacted on equal rights issues in Britain. He was assassinated in 1968.

A whole nation watched men land on the moon in 1969, then a year later followed with hearts in their mouths as Apollo 13 limped home from its aborted moon mission (1970). Flying abroad for holidays became very popular and cheap. The world was opening up.

The 1970s

This decade represented the 'hangover' from the sixties. The economy collapsed, strike action wrecked the basic functioning of society and jobs were harder to come by. In Northern Ireland the troubles entered a more violent phase. The UK voted to join the Common Market (1971). The Sex Discrimination Act was passed in 1975, and the Race Relations Act the following year.

The silicon microchip was invented in 1971, a small invention that would lead to a dramatic technological advance. On a different scientific note, the first test-tube baby was born in 1978.

The 1980s

This was the beginning of the fully fledged Thatcher years. Unions were controlled, some would argue emasculated. Computers became the medium of the future. Microwaves found their way into homes, along with videos. Individualism, capitalism and materialism were to be the mantras of this period. AIDS was discovered. The first fax was sent in 1980.

Ironically, the Falklands war opened the decade. A wave of patriotism or perhaps jingoism swept through the country, carrying the Conservatives back into power the following year.

The 1990s

The age of technology really impacted on every aspect of life – computers, e-mail, mobile phones, digital television, play stations, CCTV, DNA testing, gene therapy, cloning. At the same time BSE shattered faith in the Government and in scientific experts, and wrecked the meat produce market.

A Labour government was swept to power in 1997 in a landslide victory. Devolution was undertaken and the Millennium Dome built. The National Lottery was created, making many more millionaires and raising money for Government and charitable projects. The decade concluded with the Millennium celebrations.

UNIT: How has life changed since 1930?

Enquiry questions	Learning objectives	Teaching activities	Learning outcomes	Literacy links	Cross-curricular links
What has happened since 1930?	• Know some of the events that altered life since 1930. • Be able to identify and select the most significant change and justify that choice. • Become interested in finding out more about this period.	Highlight key changes over the period, especially national events, technology and medicine and social history. Match events and decades. Write report and select most important change. Justify. Visit to a museum.	Children: • name and date several key events causing change • write about a significant change or event	Look at books and famous children's authors from the period.	Music: explore popular music from the decades and major British composers such as Britten and Walton.
How do I research an aspect of life since 1930?	• Know how to find out about the aspect selected. • Know what the key questions of the enquiry are. • Be able to plan a research enquiry with a partner. • Use secondary and primary sources of information to find out about the aspect.	Independent research using key questions, timeline and description of specific changes. Use of secondary sources (information books, CD-ROMs and Internet) and primary sources (photographs, written accounts, maps, directories, oral evidence, film archive). Gather eye-witness data from family and friends.	• plan independent research enquiry • identify key questions to direct enquiry • select and use primary and secondary sources • make notes accurately summarising reading	Skimming, scanning and reading for meaning, use of index and contents, subheadings and captions. Summarising text for key information.	PSHE: working collaboratively, communicating effectively.
What can our families tell us about the past?	• Be able to formulate questions that can provide eye-witness information. • Find out about the past from eye-witnesses. • Understand that eye-witness evidence is personal and cannot be generalised.	In pairs children discuss what sort of information they want to find out. Formulate appropriate questions to be used in gathering information from at least four people.	• formulate questions to gather information • realise that we cannot generalise	Writing for a purpose.	
How can we present our research?	• Be able to choose the most suitable ways of presenting information. • Be able to use a range of 2-D, 3-D and electronic means of presenting information. • Be sufficiently confident in their subject knowledge to answer individual questions and explain.	Consider how to present the information they have gathered for a display. Prepare their displays. Open day for parents and guests. Children stand by to answer questions. School assembly on change during the decades.	• know about an aspect of life since 1930 and to be able to answer questions • present information in an accessible form using appropriate method		Maths: data handling and presentation, accurate use of timeline. Design and technology: model-making to convey information. PSHE: welcome visitors and talk confidently with them; be proud of their achievements and feel good about themselves.
What has stayed the same and what will happen in the future?	• Understand that despite change through time there are core needs that represent continuity. • Be able to name some of those core needs. • Be able to predict likely future trends in relation to their research aspect.	Give examples of major change between 1930 and now. Consider what has stayed the same during that time. Consider the future. What changes are likely to happen? Work on 'future' display.	• realise that whilst some things change other basic needs stay the same • predict probable change in the future.		Art: display about life in the future.

What has happened since 1930?

What you need and preparation
Have ready the class timeline and labels for key events, such as the Jarrow Hunger March, Declaration of War, VE Day, VJ Day, Festival of Britain, Korean War, moon landing, UK entry into Common Market, Falklands War. Prepare copies of photocopiable pages 120 to 122 for each child.

What to do

5 mins **Introduction**
Introduce the topic and tell the children that they are going to find out some of the key events and changes that have happened since 1930.

45 mins **Development**
Using the class timeline, ask the children if they know of any major events that happened in the period, or any important decades. Record the key events on the timeline.

Add any major events that they have missed out, decade by decade, starting with the thirties and working forwards. Focus on three main aspects – technological, social and national/international events. Distribute copies of photocopiable page 120 for the children's reference.

Next give the children copies of the worksheet on photocopiable page 121 and ask them to consider what they think has been the most important or significant change over these seventy years. Children can then work individually to match events to decades on photocopiable page 122.

10 mins **Plenary**
Place the key events and changes on the timeline together. Ask the children to justify their choice of something as a 'key event'. Explain that in the next session, they will be doing some paired research on a chosen aspect of life since 1930. This will lead to a display and an open day.

Give the class a list of potential themes: clothes and fashion, childhood, schooling, sport, popular music, entertainment, food and drink, toys and games, shops, homes, flight, land transport, inventions, communications technology, scientific developments, medicine and health, weapons and warfare, law and order, cultural diversity, famous people. Ask them to note down their choice of a possible partner and a first, second and third choice of research topic.

Differentiation
Sit with children of lower ability to assist with the worksheet.
More able children could be asked to prioritise the key events in order of historical significance.

Assessing learning outcomes
Can the children identify very important events or changes and justify their selection? Can they match events to the right decade?

How do I research an aspect of life since 1930?

What you need and preparation
Have available substantial supplies of information books, primary sources of evidence (for example directories, maps, newspapers, photographs) and access to computer software and the Internet. Decide how you are going to organise access to these sources. You will need access to a board or flipchart. Make sure there is plenty of paper available for note-taking. Make a copy of photocopiable pages 123 and 124 for each child.

How has life changed since 1930?

Learning objectives
● Know how to find out about the aspect selected.
● Know what the key questions of the enquiry are.
● Be able to plan a research enquiry with a partner.
● Use secondary and primary sources of information to find out about the aspect.

Lesson organisation
Whole class, with teacher-led input; pairs working on research and planning; pairs reviewing progress and making further plans.

Vocabulary
research enquiry
key questions
primary and secondary sources of information
aspect

ICT opportunities
● Create a web page on the school site.

What to do

Introduction
15 mins Allocate the topics and the research pairs based on the information gained in the plenary session of the last activity. Reiterate the task and the time frame, reminding children that they are going to produce a display on their allocated aspect. This will include a 'key events and changes' timeline, pictures, models and writing. They will also produce a brief summary of changes and put it onto an information website or disk for general school use.

Explain about the choices of potential sources of information. List these on the board. Explain the organisation and access to the source material. If necessary, remind the children how to skim, scan, use index and contents pages and take notes. Give out copies of the 'Getting started' information sheets on photocopiable pages 123 and 124 to each child. Work through the information with the class, and explain about the use of key questions.

Development
40 mins Let the children work in their pairs to decide on their key questions, and then start to make notes from secondary information books and primary sources. Monitor the children's use of the resource materials to ensure fair access.

Plenary
5 mins In pairs, let the children consider what they have achieved and what they want to do at the next session. Ask them to record this in their notes.

Differentiation
Pairs should be, if possible, mixed-ability, especially where one is a less confident reader. Support and help structure research for any lower- ability pairs (for example markers in information books, access to only one or two information books). Help them choose questions and organise the research as necessary. More able children can have access to a wider range of resource materials.

Assessing learning outcomes
Have the pairs identified sensible key questions? Are the pairs capable of cooperating together? Are the children able to organise their time and effort to find out information? Are the children extracting and summarising appropriate information?

30 mins What can our families tell us about the past?

Learning objectives
● Be able to formulate questions in order to find out about the past from eye-witnesses.

Lesson organisation
Teacher-led, with whole-class input; pairs; teacher-led, with whole class input.

What you need and preparation
Prepare multiple copies of photocopiable page 125 (four to six copies per pair). Children will need writing materials.

What to do

Introduction
20 mins Explain the value of asking questions of people who were alive during the period being studied. Talk about how because the period under investigation is recent, there are plenty of people who are able to tell us what things were like. Explain that this is called primary evidence.

Development
5 mins Ask the children to work in their research pairs. Give them copies of the questionnaires on photocopiable page 125. Get them to spend a few minutes talking about the key questions

they want to ask, based on work from the previous session, making sure that they agree. Explain that they will need to write in their agreed questions on the questionnaire sheet to ask people of different ages. If possible, the questionnaires should be directed towards at least four people, preferably who were children in the 1930s, 1950s, 1970s and 1980s.

5 mins Plenary
Explain that information could be gathered by e-mail, telephone or post, or in a face-to-face interview, and that the children will have to write down the answers to these questions. Remind them that any information gathered reflects one person's experience and that not everyone would have lived the same life. Stress that we cannot generalise.

Differentiation
Help children of lower ability with writing out questions if needed.

Assessing learning outcomes
Were the children capable of formulating appropriate questions? Did they manage to gather useful accounts for their topic?

Vocabulary
eye-witness
account
questionnaire
personal
generalised

**ICT
opportunities**
Use e-mail to
gather information.

**Follow-up
activity**
Ask the children to
gather the evidence
as a homework
assignment.

1 hour How can we present our research?

What you need and preparation
Organise access to computers for word-processing and data presentation. Prepare a booking-in sheet for use of the computer terminals. Have available supplies of good quality paper, coloured paper, felt-tipped pens, crayons, paints and modelling materials. Provide display boards with clear divisions for each pair's work. Prepare copies of photocopiable page 126 (enough for one between two).

What to do

10 mins Introduction
Explain that the next three or four sessions will be devoted to the writing-up of information gained from the eye-witness questionnaires and other research activities undertaken by the research partners. Children will also prepare items for the display and input data on the computer. Remind the pairs that their work must include a timeline with key events or changes, a report discussing the most important changes in this aspect over the last 70 years, and a short entry on the computer file or web page.

Explain the display allocation, making sure each pair knows which part of the display is for their material, and discuss the possible ways in which the material could be presented (for example written, pictorial, graphs, models, etc).

45 mins Development
Hand out the 'Presenting your research' sheets from photocopiable page 126 to each pair. Explain that this will help them in structuring their material for the display. Tell the children to work carefully through the sections together, then start on their design and begin their presentation work.

5 mins Plenary
Get the children to tidy away their display work before discussing in pairs their plans for the following session.

**Learning
objectives**
• Be able to present
the most suitable
ways of presenting
information.
• Be able to use a
range of 2D, 3D and
electronic means of
presenting
information.
• Be sufficiently
confident in their
subject knowledge
to answer individual
questions and
explain.

**Lesson
organisation**
Teacher-led
followed by pair
work

Vocabulary
presentation
timeline

**ICT
opportunities**
Children can input
information onto a
file or web page, and
develop their word-
processing and data
handling skills.

CHAPTER 2
BRITAIN SINCE 1930

How has life changed since 1930?

Differentiation

Support pairs of lower ability in organisation. More able children can be allowed to work with minimum supervision.

Assessing learning outcomes

Can the children select appropriate ways of presenting their information? Can they summarise the information from their notes? Do they demonstrate sound knowledge of the changes and events related to their allocated aspect of this topic?

Follow-up activities
● Children can finish their presentation work, then organise an open day with guests, parents and other pupils seeing the display and asking questions.
● They could organise an assembly about change, possibly focusing on fashion and music.

(2 hours) What has stayed the same and what will happen in the future?

Learning objectives
● Understand that despite change through time there are core needs that represent continuity.
● Be able to name some of those core needs.
● Be able to predict likely future trends in relation to their research aspect.

Lesson organisation
Teacher-led input with whole class, then small group discussion and feedback; work in pairs; feedback from pairs to whole class.

Vocabulary
continuity
core needs
the future
prediction

ICT opportunities
Children can learn to use the scanner.

What you need and preparation

Provide A5 paper and felt-tipped pens for each small group, and a range of materials suitable for making a display. Have ready black backing paper, a display board and a staple gun. Have available a camera and a computer with a scanner. You will need access to a board or flipchart.

What to do

(20 mins) Introduction

Ask one or two children to give examples of the great changes that have happened during the past 70 years. Then ask the class if anything has stayed the same during this time. Give an example of a core need, such as a need for housing. Explain the term 'core need' and tell the class that it means essential needs that do not change with time. Ask the children to work in small mixed- ability groups to come up with other core needs that remain the same, regardless of the historical period (employment, healthcare, education, food, sanitation, etc).

After 15 minutes, invite groups to give feedback to the whole class. Record this on the board.

(90 mins) Development

Ask the children to sit in their research pairs. Introduce the idea of predicting the future trends. What do they think life will be like in 20 years hence? Ask the pairs to come up with some ideas then feed back one idea to the whole class. Write their ideas up on the board, then allocate a different one to each pair.

After feedback, draw up a rough plan for a display on the board, based on ideas from the children. For example, it could be a street scene, or a more abstract design such as a central word 'Future' or '2020' surrounded by 15 satellite ovals or circles. Explain that each pair is going to prepare a picture representing that change they have identified. Show them the range of materials available for their display work.

Spend the rest of the time with children producing their display material.

(10 mins) Plenary

Take a photograph of the display, then one of the whole class. Explain that these will be scanned into the computer and put with the topic web page or the research file. A hard copy will be printed off and stored in the archives of the school for a class in the year 2020 to examine and see if they were right.

Assessing learning outcomes

Can the children give examples of core needs that represent the continuity in history? Can they predict a future change in relation to their researched aspect? Can they design an illustration to represent that future change?

Ancient Greece

The study of Ancient Greece has remained a compulsory part of the History National Curriculum since it was first introduced in 1991. The most recent update of the History Orders makes it clear that one of the purposes of studying this topic is to look at the influence this ancient civilisation continues to have on the world today. However, this statement is seen as controversial by some – it has been pointed point out that the Ancient Greeks were in turn heavily influenced by other non-European cultures which existed at the same time, such as those in Egypt and other parts of Africa, India and Persia. The ancestors of the Greeks belonged to the great Indo-European family of peoples, which spread out from the Caucasus into India, Iran and Europe. They began to enter Greece from the north about 1900BC. The more we find out about the past, the more we realise that the Ancient Greek 'civilisation' was far from unique.

At one time the history of Greece and Rome was given the title of 'classical' and the study of Greek and Latin was seen as crucial in a 'gentleman's education'. (Ladies and lesser mortals of both sexes had to survive without such an education!) There are probably two major reasons for its place in the primary school today. Firstly because several aspects of Greek culture have informed life in Europe over the centuries. This Greek legacy has influenced our language, architecture, drama, art, mathematics, science, medicine, politics, astronomy and philosophy. Secondly its study provides a different type of context for children to develop their historical skills.

Who were the Ancient Greeks?

'Ancient' is an important historical concept, though for many children 'ancient' is a word used to describe most adults! Less able children should be able to grasp that 'ancient' in the context of this unit is a very long time ago. They need to understand that they will not find an 'ancient' Greek wandering about in Greece today and that some 'ancient' Greeks were children like themselves. For children of average and higher ability there is a need to come to some understanding about 'ancient' linked with the word 'civilisation'. The fundamental reason that this unit has remained part of the statutory curriculum for primary children is that this ancient civilisation is seen to have some importance about the way in which our own culture has developed. Ancient Greece is part of our history. Our second unit explores this in more depth, but this unit enables children to find out about the lives of the ordinary Ancient Greeks as well as of some of the more famous.

Children need to be able to place the area of Greece on a modern map. They need to understand that limited amounts of farm land in Ancient Greece meant that as the population increased people had to leave their home in order to find new land. As long ago as the 8th and 7th centuries BC the Greeks had established themselves as far as the Black Sea, North Africa, Italy and Spain. These migrations have obvious similarities with movements of other peoples over time and if children have studied the Romans, Anglo-Saxons and/or Vikings, there are comparisons which can be made.

Ancient Greece - the time

Few primary-school pupil texts go beyond a very light touch of the chronology of Ancient Greece because an in-depth study of several thousand years of Greek culture and politics would be totally inappropriate for primary pupils. However, more able readers may come across adult texts, CD-ROM and Internet sites which make mention of the different periods of Greek civilisation. These are:

> ***Pre-Homeric and Homeric*** – From earliest times to c.700BC
> ***Archaic*** – c.700BC to 479BC
> ***Classical*** – c.479BC to 404BC
> ***Hellenistic*** – c.404BC to 146BC

Most pupil texts concentrate on the classical period. This is deemed to start with the consolidation of the power of Athens after Salamis and Plataea and finish with its surrender to the Spartans at the end of the Peloponnesian War. It is often called the golden age of Greece, because of recorded evidence of its arts and learning, and is linked almost entirely to Athens itself.

This is a challenging, but rewarding unit. It is suggested that it starts with a 'pre-lesson' display on the Ancient Greeks, to give children an opportunity to activate their background knowledge of the topic and stimulate them to make some initial discoveries by themselves.

UNIT: Who were the Ancient Greeks?

Enquiry questions	Learning objectives	Teaching activities	Learning outcomes	Literacy links	Cross-curricular links
What do we know about the Ancient Greeks and what more do we want to know about them?	• Be able to locate Greece and UK on a world map. • Demonstrate and record existing knowledge about the Ancient Greeks. • Use key words to ask relevant questions about Ancient Greece. • Identify relevant sources of information to answer questions. • Know about Greece as geographical location.	Pre-lesson display on Ancient Greeks. Identify what is already known. Record additional questions.	Children: • have background knowledge of the topic • are interested in the Ancient Greeks	Obtaining information from text and posters.	Geography: use of atlas.
What did people look like in Ancient Greece?	• Be able to find pictures of Ancient Greeks in non-fiction texts and identify those that would be useful in answering question. • Know what sort of clothing was worn by Ancient Greeks. • Be able to give historical explanations for differences in clothing. • Evaluate the source material from which their evidence is drawn.	Use illustration of Greek boy and girl to make inventory of clothes. Ask questions about how we know what they wore. Identify and evaluate differences between clothing worn by Ancient Greeks and children today.	• know what clothes people wore in Ancient Greece • record information and reasons can support learning from a variety of visual sources • raise questions about validity of source material	Visual literacy.	Geography: climatic conditions. Science: considering evidence and evaluating; materials and their properties.
How did ordinary people live?	• Decide on a particular aspect to research. • Raise historical questions related to that aspect of life. • Identify appropriate resource material • Consolidate work on note-taking.	Return to initial questions and identify those relating to daily life: housing, transport, education, language, games, work, religion. Explore variety of sources to find out more information about one chosen aspect. Model note-taking to identify key words in texts and visual sources.	• use a variety of sources to investigate initial questions • use independent fact-finding and interpretation of data	Gaining information from non-fiction texts.	Maths: negative numbers (timeline).
Who were some famous Ancient Greeks?	• Be able to recount a brief life history of a famous person from Ancient Greece. • Know the difference between biography, legend and myth. • Be able to place a person on a timeline.	Find out names of some famous Greeks that they have come across in reading or from general knowledge. Fact/myth/legend. Investigate lives of some of these. Place in chronological order and explain about the 'invisible' people in Ancient Greek history – women and slaves.	• know that there were a number of famous Greeks • become aware of the limited information about groups of people such as women and slaves	Gaining information from non-fiction texts.	Geography: expansion of Greek Empire.
Was all of Ancient Greece the same?	• Understand the difficulties of looking at a whole country as one entity. • Use historical sources to explore differences between Athens and Sparta. • Identify difficulties of the interpretation of historical sources when victors write history.	Map of Greece – differences between Athens and Sparta. Compile list of similarities and differences. Explain possible bias in history.	• explore differences between Athens and Sparta.		Geography: how location can influence peoples views. Citizenship: rules within different communities.

CHAPTER 3
ANCIENT GREECE

Who were the Ancient Greeks?

 What do we know about the Ancient Greeks and what more do we want to know about them?

Background information

This unit aims to build on the children's existing knowledge of the Ancient Greeks. It is unlikely that many children will be aware of their own knowledge, so create a display of books and posters to give them an opportunity to find out that the Ancient Greeks lived long ago, lived in a place where the weather was very different from the UK, and this place still exists today. This is the starting point for the K point in the learning grid below – what knowledge do children bring to the subject? Move children from this point to what they want to find out about the Ancient Greeks – the W point in the learning grid. The activities then provide the substance for the third section of the grid – the L point.

What do we know about the Ancient Greeks and what more do we want to know?		
K What do we already know?	W What do we want to know?	L What have we learnt?

What you need and preparation

Make a display from all the relevant resources to be used in the unit – posters (including a map of Ancient Greece showing Athens, Sparta and Marathon), non-fiction texts, CD-ROM(s), artefacts and a world map. If a local museum has information on Ancient Greece, they might be able to provide an information sheet. Prepare and display a large sheet of paper headed 'What do we know about the Ancient Greeks?' Collect together travel brochures of Greece containing simple maps. Provide a variety of texts containing maps of Ancient Greece that children can use for tracing, writing materials and tracing paper. Make copies of photocopiable page 127 for each child. Prior to the lesson, draw children's attention to the display and encourage them to respond to the initial question and browse through relevant CD-ROMs and websites. Find out if any children have ever been to Greece and, if so, ask them to bring in any souvenirs, and so on. Make sure you have access to a board or flipchart.

What to do

40 mins Introduction

Identify the lesson objectives – either on the board or verbally. Ask the children what they already know about this topic. Record their responses on the board. Model note-taking with key words (mainly verbs and nouns), rather than full sentences.

Redirect children's attention to the display for any additional information they can gather from covers of books and posters. If necessary, model how to obtain information from texts and posters.

Give children ten minutes to record any key information and key questions on individual copies of photocopiable page 127, giving support to those needing it.

40 mins Development

Identify the key questions the class will need to answer if they want to know more. Record these on the board. Model writing a full question with a question mark. Children should be encouraged to come up with the questions themselves. If necessary, write the key question words on board – who, what, why, when, how, which. Add any questions that the children overlook.

Give the children five minutes to pick three key questions. Ensure that at least one relates to everyday life and one to famous people.

Find a child who has asked 'Where was Ancient Greece?' Get the child to read the question to the whole class, then together find the UK and then Greece on a modern world map. Explain that the unit they are going to be studying is about a people who lived a very long time ago. Introduce the word 'Ancient' and make comparisons with the Ancient Egyptians if appropriate. Explain that one reason why we study the Ancient Greeks is because they conquered a lot of other people. Look at the poster map of Ancient Greece. Make comparisons between the size of Greece today and Ancient Greece. Identify this as a future objective – how did Ancient Greece become so large? (Comparisons could be made with the Roman Empire, if children have studied the Romans.) Draw a rough timeline showing the Ancient Egyptians, Greeks and Romans if appropriate.

Demonstrate to children the skill of tracing a map, then let them trace a map of Ancient Greece from a non-fiction text and mark on Athens, Sparta, Marathon, Troy, and the Aegean and Mediterranean Seas.

10 mins **Plenary**

Ask the children if they have thought of any additional questions. Record these on the board. Then ask them where they are likely to find the answers to the questions they have asked. Encourage them to move beyond the non-fiction texts in the classroom to searching the Internet, CD-ROMs, the local library, local museum, and so on.

Differentiation

Less able children should be given inconspicuous help with 'reading the display' prior to the session, so they have some facts about the Ancient Greeks to hand for the whole-class session. Offer support for children on individual tasks such as recording questions and tracing simple maps. Rather than tracing the map of Ancient Greece, less able children could trace a simple modern map from a tourist brochure for comparison with those produced by the rest of the class.

More able children could move beyond simple questions and draw on cause and effect (for example did the position of Ancient Greece have an influence on its Empire?). If appropriate, they could also be asked to find out approximate dates for the Egyptian and Roman civilisations and the extent of their Empires for comparison.

Assessing learning outcomes

Can the children find the UK, Greece and Athens on a world map? Can they find Athens, Sparta and Marathon on a map of Ancient Greece? Can they identify any facts they know about the Ancient Greeks? Are they interested in finding out answers to at least one of the questions they have set themselves? Can they identify two sources of information which will help them answer the questions? Can they identify some links between other historical periods they have studied?

ICT opportunities
Use the Internet as a historical source.

Follow-up activity
Find additional sources of information about the Ancient Greeks. This could include talking to older children, who have already studied Ancient Greece. Record the sources in the third column of photocopiable page 127. Encourage children to write specific titles, relevant page numbers and website addresses, rather than just writing 'books' and 'Internet'.

What did people look like in Ancient Greece?

Background information

The paintings on Ancient Greek vases reveal a variety of clothing worn by the Ancient Greeks. The vases show changes in fashion over the years as well as differences between social classes. The basic article of clothing for both men and women was a tunic, known as a chiton, which was made from a rectangular piece of cloth. Women generally wore it full length, while most younger men wore it just above their knees. Men did wear longer tunics on ceremonial occasions.

Wealthy men and women also wore cloaks, hats and shoes. However, because of the heat, cloaks were sometimes worn by men without a tunic underneath. The majority of people would have gone barefoot.

Who were
the Ancient
Greeks?

Learning objectives
● Be able to find pictures of Ancient Greeks in non-fiction texts and identify those that would be useful in answering this question.
● Know what sort of clothing was worn by the Ancient Greeks.
● Be able to give historical explanations for differences in clothing.
● Evaluate the source material from which their evidence is drawn.

Lesson organisation
Whole-class overview, then individual and paired working; whole class, then individual and/or paired work; whole class.

Vocabulary
ancient
chiton
primary
secondary
sources of evidence

What you need and preparation

Have available a good variety of non-fiction texts and posters which show Ancient Greek clothing. Make sure that some vase paintings are included with these. Ensure that all children can see both the photographs of primary source material and the artists' illustrations. Place the tables or desks into groups, so that children can work collaboratively with a variety of different non-fiction texts. Prepare a 'chiton' by cutting an old sheet in half, and fastening it with safety pins, and rope for a belt. Display a map of the Ancient Greek Empire. Write on the board 'What did the Ancient Greeks wear?' Prepare copies of photocopiable page 128 for each child. Provide writing and drawing materials.

What to do

30 mins **Introduction**
Briefly introduce the lesson by reminding the children of the questions they asked in the last session and highlighting today's question as one of these. Challenge children to find at least three different pictures or illustrations of Ancient Greeks, which show what type of clothes they wore. Then ask them to make brief sketches of two different types of clothing, including footwear, headgear and adornments. Children should be encouraged to comment on the differences between illustrations in different books and speculate about reasons for this.

45 mins **Development**
Ask the children what sort of pictures they have found and list these on the board. These should include pictures on vases, coins, colour photographs of people dressed in Ancient Greek costume (possibly from films or television programmes), and illustrations from information texts. Explain the difference between primary and secondary source material (if this has not already been covered) and ask the children to identify the primary source material on the list. Underline these on the board. Challenge the children's thinking by asking questions. Is a photograph of a real vase a primary or secondary source? Is a replica a primary or secondary source? Encourage the children to justify their responses. Point out the differences between a photograph of an artefact and the real thing. What information can you not get from a photograph (size, front and back view)?

Children who have found nudes on pictures of Greek vases should be told that there was a special reason for this. Ask them if they can find out what it was (give a clue that it was linked to Olympic Games).

Ask plenty of questions to stimulate the children's thinking. What sources of evidence are we most likely to see today in museums (models of buildings, pottery, vases, coins, and so on)? What is the problem about finding clothes worn by people in the past (decay of many clothing materials)? What do illustrators use to draw pictures in non-fiction texts? What difficulties do they have (not everyone wore the same clothes, clothes changed over time, the colour of the fabric is often absent in vase paintings)? What did the people look like? What difference does the climate make to people's appearance (browner skin, lighter clothing)? Did the Greeks' views about women affect their clothing (women often covered their heads – often more obvious on vases than in illustrations)?

Look at a map of Ancient Greece, showing the expanded Empire. What difference would this have made on their clothing? Is this represented in the books they have in front of them? Why not?

If appropriate, explore the partial nature and bias of historical evidence, reinforcing the lack of evidence and our heavy dependence on the 'media' of the time, for example vases. Can children link this with the media exposure of fashion today?

Let the children work individually to complete photocopiable page 128.

Plenary

15 mins Dress one child in a chiton. Discuss the likely underwear, footwear and headgear that would have been worn with it. Can the class think of any difficulties in wearing something like this (warmth, ease of movement)? Ask if this is a primary or secondary source of evidence. Make links with the points made about primary and secondary source material on the photocopiable sheet.

Ask children if they can think of any other aspects of daily life which would be difficult to find out about because of lack of primary source material (for example furnishings, lives of slaves and poorer people).

Differentiation

Less able children could be involved in the dressing-up in a chiton activity, while more able children could try to find out about the type of materials used, the colour of dyes, and so on, and make notes. Tell them just to use key words, for example fabric – wool, later silk; dyed red, yellow, blue or green; some patterns.

Assessing learning outcomes

Can children describe what one form of clothing might have looked like in Ancient Greece? Can they identify three sources of evidence we have about what people looked like and what they wore? Are they able to give a reason why some evidence from the past is difficult to find?

How did ordinary people live?

 (1 hour 30 mins)

Background information

Most Greeks lived in houses made from mud bricks. Richer people would have built on a stone base. Poorer Greeks lived in a small box-like home with few windows and a single door opening onto a street. Houses in the towns often had more than one storey and larger ones had courtyards with an altar for family prayers.

Women were responsible for running the house and domestic slaves would do most of the work in wealthy households. They collected water from the well and this is often depicted on vase paintings. Pottery ovens for cooking bread and charcoal fires for cooking meat and vegetables have also been found.

What you need and preparation

Have available a good supply of relevant texts and posters, at appropriate levels for different abilities, plus access to CD-ROMs and websites. Make copies of photocopiable pages 129 (one per group) and 130 (optional). Prior to the lesson, identify suitable working groups of three and which aspects of daily life can be researched most easily from the resources available. Prepare topic cards for each group to identify what particular aspect they are researching, for example education, homes, slaves, work, sports, food, transport. For each group, provide strips of card and felt-tipped pens. They should also have access to presentation materials, for example acetates and pens for use with an overhead projector; *PowerPoint* if available. Have some Blu-Tack available. You will need access to a board or flipchart.

What to do

Introduction

20 mins On the board, model note-taking from a history text to the whole class.

Return to the original list of questions from the first session. Identify those which would give us

Learning objectives
● Decide on a particular aspect to research.
● Raise historical questions related to that aspect of life.
● Identify appropriate resource material.
● Consolidate work on note-taking.

Lesson organisation
Whole class; groups of three working on different aspects, with adult support where necessary; group presentations to whole class.

Vocabulary
archaeological evidence

more information about daily life. (How did people move about? What were schools like? What were houses like? What work did people do? What was life like for girls or boys?) Identify with the children specific topics for research in order to find out more about how the Ancient Greeks lived. Give the groups topic cards to remind them of their focus for research. Point out possible links between questions and index entries. For example, 'What was life like for girls?' could be linked to possible index headings such as 'Education', 'Home life' and 'Women'. Make brief comparisons with life today where possible. For example, How do you get to school? What other forms of transport do we have? What would have been available to the Ancient Greeks?

Explain that at the end of the session you will invite groups from each topic area to make a presentation, so that by the end of the session everyone will know more. Stress that each presentation must include one new word connected with the Ancient Greeks, three points of information about that aspect and a quiz question for other children to answer. The quiz question should be written on a strip of card with a felt-tipped pen. Distribute copies of photocopiable page 129 and explain how it could be used to help with the presentations.

Recap on the research skills used in the last lesson on Greek clothing, and write them up on the board:
● reference skills such as structural guiders (title, index, contents, glossary)
● skimming and scanning skills, picking out only the relevant information without reading everything
● think where the author has got their information from
● use more than one source of information to cross-check (are there differences in information in different books?)
● make notes, rather than copy out chunks of the book.

40 mins Development
As the children work in their groups, monitor their:
● skill in suggesting other questions to ask about the same topic
● ability to locate a relevant source of information
● skill in using structural guiders, skimming and scanning text with confidence
● interest and involvement in the topic
● justification for noting down information
● using note form as modelled
● making oral comparisons between now and then
● making comparisons with other texts.

Collect the quiz questions five minutes before the plenary and attach them on to the wall. Ensure that each group has collected three pieces of information about their aspect and has recorded these either on photocopiable page 129 or on an overhead.

30 mins Plenary
Choose one group from each of the topic areas to make a presentation. If time, go through the quiz questions orally.

Differentiation
Supply texts at different levels.

Assessing learning outcomes
Can children identify additional questions within their chosen topic? Can they find relevant information from the texts and visual sources to supply answers to questions set? Can they record this in note form, rather than copy from the text? Can they discuss differences in presentation and information between the texts – moving towards evaluation of a text?

ICT opportunities
Use *PowerPoint* for presentation and for researching for information.

Follow-up activities
● Have a class quiz to answer all the questions.
● Give out copies of photocopiable page 130 and ask children to use it to research other areas of daily life in Ancient Greece.

 # Who were some famous Ancient Greeks?

Background information

Alexander the Great was the son of the Macedonian king, Philip II. He was one of the greatest military leaders of all time. As a child, Alexander was influenced by his teacher, the Greek philosopher Aristotle. Aristotle taught Alexander to love philosophy and Greek ways. Alexander's greatest wish was to spread the Greek legacy. To turn his wish into reality, Alexander conquered lands, built cities modelled on the Greek cities and encouraged a blend of cultures and ideas.

What you need and preparation

Have available a good account of Alexander the Great either taken from a non-fiction text or off the Internet. Display a map of Alexander's conquests and pictures of Alexander. Provide a selection of non-fiction texts and CD-ROMs about the Ancient Greeks. Prepare a 'People to know' chart, with the following names and dates: Aeschylus about 525–456BC; Alexander the Great about 356–323BC; Aristotle about 384–322BC; Herodotus about 484–425BC; Homer about 950–900BC; Pericles about 495–429BC; Socrates about 470–399BC. Prepare an enlarged copy of photocopiable page 131 (or an acetate for the overhead projector) and a copy of photocopiable page 132 for less able children. Have available card circles (about 12cm in diameter) for the children to write on, plus felt-tipped pens and paper for note-taking. You will need access to a board or flipchart.

What to do

30 mins Introduction

Review work done to date, then ask the children to note down any famous Ancient Greek person they can think of. Encourage them to use resource materials in the classroom to identify these people. Record the names on the board and ask the class whether all the people on the list really existed. Display an enlarged copy of photocopiable page 131 and work through it together. Discuss the differences between a known real person, such as Alexander, and Helen of Troy, who probably existed but is surrounded by legend, and obvious mythological characters such as Herakles (Hercules).

Look at the 'People to know' chart and point out that it is possible to find approximate dates for these people. Explain that writing about a real person is called a biography. Evaluate the chart. What do the children notice about it? (There are no women because they stayed indoors and had few opportunities.) Why are the dates only approximate? Who lived furthest back in time?

Read a simple non-fiction text about the life of Alexander the Great. Cover the key facts, and point out Macedonia on the map.

If you are using the Internet as a reference source, highlight some of the more complex language, so that children understand that many of these websites are for adults who are interested in Alexander the Great. They do, however, contain some very useful visual sources and animations of Alexander's journey.

40 mins Development

Invite the children to research some of the people on the chart, or to research individuals of their own choice. Remind them that the key purpose of this activity is to find out why these people are famous today. Give them the card circles and tell them to write on the approximate dates of birth and death, reasons why that person is famous, plus any other interesting facts (Figure 1). Then ask them to arrange their cards in chronological order according to the approximate date of birth.

Figure 1

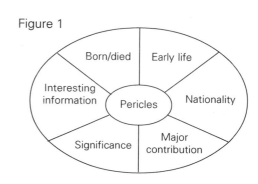

Learning objectives
- Be able to recount a brief life history of a famous person from Ancient Greece, showing reasons why this person was famous.
- Know the difference between biography, legend and myth.
- Be able to place a person on a timeline.

Lesson organisation
Whole class, with teacher modelling the activity; individuals; whole class.

Vocabulary
myth
legend
hero
biography

ICT opportunities
Use an Internet search to find websites linked with Alexander the Great. Download a map of his journey, photographs of coins, statues and so on. Compile a list of useful websites for Alexander.

CHAPTER 3
ANCIENT GREECE

Who were the Ancient Greeks?

Follow-up activity
Research reasons why Alexander and his army were so successful in conquering so many different peoples. Explain that he often named cities after himself, then ask children to find some of these on a map. Can they find out after what animal he named the city of Bucephalus?

20 mins Plenary
Ask the children to choose any one person they have researched. Then ask who has the person who lived furthest back in time. Ask a child with the relevant card to come out and stand at the front. Continue inviting children out to the front and standing them in order to form a human timeline. Ask the children who are still seated to say why each person was famous.

Differentiation
Less able children could be provided with the worksheet on photocopiable page 132, based on information covered in the session, while the rest of the class carry out research into other historical figures.

For more able children, increase the number of famous person cards, then get them to make individual timelines with them.

Assessing learning outcomes
Are the children able to distinguish between a mythical person and a real one? Can they use texts effectively and with interest to find information about birth and death dates and facts about real people from the past? Are they able to evaluate the usefulness of the texts? How certain are children when working with BC chronology?

 Was all of Ancient Greece the same?

Learning objectives
• Understand the difficulties of looking at a whole country as one entity.
• Use historical sources to explore differences between Athens and Sparta.
• Identify difficulties of the interpretation of historical sources when the victors write history.

Background information
Ancient Greece was divided into states. Athens and Sparta were two of these city states and were governed quite differently.

Athens was a 'democracy', although not in the way that we think of democracies. For those who could be citizens, citizenship involved heavy duties and responsibilities. For example, an Athenian citizen found in the market place while an assembly was being held was branded with red paint. In this way people knew that he had been avoiding his responsibilities. Positions of power in Athens rotated annually. Every year nearly a fifth of the adult male citizens took their turn to be judges, public officials and council members. Most of the jobs were part-time because it was recognised that citizens had their own work to do as farmers.

Sparta had hereditary kings and was effectively an oligarchy because of the difficulty of becoming a citizen. To be a citizen, Spartans needed to prove their descent from the original inhabitants of Sparta. They also had to submit to the education and discipline imposed on them and be a member of the military masses. Boys who fulfilled the initial regulations for Spartan citizenship left home when they were seven to be trained as soldiers. Unlike girls in other Greek states, girls in Sparta were encouraged to participate in sports such as running, wrestling and ball games.

What you need and preparation
Have available non-fiction texts on Ancient Greece and computer-based resources. Prepare copies of photocopiable page 133 for less able children. Display a large map of Ancient Greece with Athens and Sparta marked clearly. Provide children with writing materials, and ensure you have access to a board or flipchart.

What to do
20 mins Introduction
Explain to the children that as Ancient Greece grew, it was dominated by two powerful communities – Athens and Sparta. In the lesson today, the children are going to find out about

these two communities and how they had different ideas about almost everything, and how they became fierce rivals.

Point out the difficulties of saying that all the people who live in the same country are alike. They may not even have the same weather. Think about the weather forecast, and how when the weather in London is hot, it may be pouring with rain somewhere else.

Look at the map of Ancient Greece and identify the differences between the location of Athens and Sparta. Athens was on a peninsula and so was able to use its location near the sea to grow as a centre of trade. It expanded overseas, whereas Sparta could only expand by conquering the city states around it. This may have accounted for many of the other differences between the cities as well.

Divide the class into two groups. Explain that one group is going to be the Spartans and will have to argue that they have a better way of life in Sparta; the other group will be the Athenians and they have to argue that their way of life is better.

(40 mins) Development

Give the children access to the research materials to find out all they can about their allocated city state. Encourage them to identify characteristics they like and dislike. (Obviously when they come to arguing why their city state is better they need to gloss over the dislikes.) Point out that viewpoints might be different, depending on whether you were a boy or girl (girls appear to have had much more freedom in Sparta than in Athens) or a slave.

Some children may choose to do this as a narrative: 'I am a girl living in Sparta. I am pleased that I don't live in Athens because…'

(30 mins) Plenary

Draw the class together. Ask an Athenian to state what Athens has to offer and why they are glad to live there. Record the plus points on the board. Ask other Athenians to add any additional reasons. Then ask the Spartans for their views and record them on the board. Ask Spartans to comment on some statements recorded by the Athenians and vice versa.

Ask the children to define what is meant by the following words: Acropolis, assembly, democracy, peninsula, city state and helot. Where would they most likely be found, i.e. in Athens, Sparta or both?

Explain that the Athenians eventually defeated the Spartans and wrote the history, so it is not surprising that Sparta sounds worse than Athens. Can children think of other circumstances where writers may not record exactly what happens because they are biased to one side (for example football matches, government reports from war zones)?

Differentiation

Let less able children use photocopiable page 133 to record some of the differences they find between Athens and Sparta. Give additional support as necessary.

Encourage more able children to imagine that they are particular individuals in the city state. Help them to understand that the views of the people in power (male citizens) might well be different from those of a girl or a slave.

Assessing learning outcomes

Do children know some of the basic differences between Athens and Sparta. Can they use some of the key vocabulary to describe the city states? Are they able to identify some of the reasons for the differences between the two states?

Lesson organisation
Whole class, divided into two groups; individual tasks; whole class.

Vocabulary
Acropolis
assembly
democracy
polis
peninsula
city state
helot

ICT opportunities
Use the computer for research purposes and for putting together presentations.

Follow-up activity
Find out what being a citizen in Athens would involve (for example having to vote).

CHAPTER 3
ANCIENT GREECE

Why is the history of Ancient Greece important to us?

Ancient Greek civilisation has influenced our language, architecture, drama, art, maths, science, medicine, politics, astronomy and philosophy. It should be remembered, however, that many of the ideas which we attribute to the Greeks were actually based on those of much older civilisations. This is particularly true when we look at ideas which were produced by Alexandrian scientists. But the Greeks were responsible for developing and spreading these ideas.

The conquest of the Persian Empire by Alexander the Great resulted in the founding of kingdoms controlled by the Greeks throughout the eastern Mediterranean. This had three major effects:

- widespread knowledge of Greek language and ideas
- the beginning of art collections and evaluation and classification of works of art
- establishment of cities, such as Alexandria in Egypt, which became major centres for learning.

The Romans also influenced the spread of Greek culture. The Romans borrowed extensively from the Greeks and the growth of the Roman Empire meant that aspects of Greek culture spread into most areas of the Empire. For example, by the 2nd century BC wealthy Romans were already collecting and copying Greek ideas and there are numerous examples of these Roman copies of Greek sculptures in museums all over the world. Children who have already studied the Romans may be able to find some useful examples of how Greek culture can be seen within the Roman civilisation.

When the Roman Empire started to collapse, Greece became a province of the eastern Byzantine Empire and the focal point of Greek life moved from Athens to Constantinople. In the centuries that followed, Greece was alternately opened and closed to travellers and interest in its legacy was sporadic.

The Grand Tour

It was not until the 17th century that the 'great travels' to Greece began. By the 18th century it had become the fashionable place for wealthy Europeans to visit. The Grand Tour undertaken by young gentlemen to complete their education often included Greece. Indeed many of the collections found in stately homes and museums today date from this period. By the Victorian period, however, there was growing concern about the 'plundering' of Greek works of art. The most famous example of this is the continuing controversy over the Elgin marbles, but many local museums have Greek artefacts that were given to them from collections made by local gentry. Children who have already studied the Victorians will be able to identify some ways in which the Ancient Greek culture influenced the Victorians, particularly Greek architecture.

The Greek legacy today

A study of Ancient Greece should leave children with some understanding of how this ancient civilisation has influenced our own history. This unit guides children through this legacy. It tackles directly the question of why we learn about ancient cultures and then looks at ways in which Greek ideas have influenced our buildings, language, literature and ideas. In order to do this properly, children need to have some understanding of who the Greeks were. Unit 1 covers this.

UNIT: Why is the history of Ancient Greece important to us?

Enquiry questions	Learning objectives	Teaching activities	Learning outcomes	Literacy links	Cross-curricular links
What do we learn from the past?	● Review vocabulary. ● Understand the purpose of studying history. ● Identify areas of our lives which carry on traditions and ideas seen in Ancient Greece. ● Identify 'asking good questions' as a skill, and part of the legacy from Greek thinkers.	What is history? Why do we learn about ancient cultures? Examine aspects of life in Ancient Greece which have relevance for us today.	Children: ● evaluate a specific area of the curriculum in terms of their own development ● identify specific areas for further investigation		PSHE and citizenship. Design and technology: evaluation of designs from the past.
How have Greek ideas influenced our buildings?	● Recognise orders of Greek architecture. ● Identify buildings which incorporate some of these ideas. ● Speculate on reasons why architects have used ideas from the past.	Look at characteristics of Greek buildings in Ancient Greece. Decide how these characteristics are reflected in local buildings Speculate as to the reasons why this has happened.	● make comparisons between buildings in Ancient Greece and local buildings		Art and design: investigate styles and traditions in local buildings; visual literacy characteristics of Greek architecture in photographs.
What stories from Ancient Greece have been handed down?	● Have a good knowledge of several Greek myths. ● Know differences between myth, legend and biography. ● Develop concept of heroes and heroines. ● Identify Greek myths in Classical paintings.	Create stories and dramas from famous Greek myths. Examine ways in which myths and legends provide explanations for natural happenings which were not understood.	● consolidate knowledge of famous Greek myths ● learn at least one new myth	English: storytelling,	Drama enactment.
How has our language been influenced by the Ancient Greeks?	● Know that many words we use today come directly from the Greeks. ● Know that many words have prefixes and suffixes of Greek origin. ● Identify words and understand that knowledge of Greek legacy in language can help with unfamiliar words. ● Recognise similarities and differences between Greek alphabet and ours today.	Find words we use which come directly from the Greek. Find parts of words which come from the Greek. Use reference texts to find additional word legacies from Ancient Greece.	● use dictionaries to find words with Greek derivations ● know key features about their own language ● know the reason for the permeation of Greek legacy within the language	English: word and sentence level work.	Art: knowledge and understanding.
How have Greek ideas influenced our understanding of citizenship?	● Consolidate previous work on Athens. ● Understand concept of citizenship in Athens. ● Define characteristics of citizenship in UK. ● Compare concept of citizenship in Ancient Greece and in UK.	Revisit work done about the organisation of Athens into a viable city state – rules, routines and regulations. Make links with 3Rs in school, at home, in the community. Use knowledge about Greek legacy in language to find out meanings of words in relation to citizenship.	● demonstrate relationship between responsibilities and rights in our society and link with Greek philosophy ● reflect on how Greek concepts of citizenship have been expanded.		PSHE and citizenship.

**Why is the
history of
Ancient Greece
important to us?**

What do we learn from the past?

(1 hour 30 mins)

Background information
The table below shows the pattern of political development in Ancient Greece and shows how the words and concepts used in this activity developed.

Monarchy
Struggle between King and nobles resulting in the King losing power

Aristocracy
Leaders of tribes and clans gradually become more oppressive and quarrel among themselves.
Several attempts made to reform sometimes resulting in

Reformers or **Lawgivers**

Where this did not work

Tyranny
When this became too harsh and cruel the tyrant was overthrown

Liberal oligarchy or **Democracy**

What you need and preparation
Prepare a word bank showing each of the words in the vocabulary section. Prior to the lesson, draw children's attention to the words in the word bank, and encourage them to find out what they mean if they do not already know. Encourage the use of glossaries in non-fiction texts. Prepare a display with the title 'The Greek legacy', incorporating children's work from the unit *Who were the Ancient Greeks?* and non-fiction texts open at pages having information on the subject. Prepare copies of photocopiable page 134 for each child. Have available a board or flip chart and large sheets of paper. Collect together some articles and photographs with captions from a local newspaper, enough for the children to have one between two.

What to do
(30 mins) Introduction
Distribute copies of photocopiable page 134 and tell the children that this is a test to review words that they encountered while studying the last unit. When they have completed the sheet, go through it together with the children marking their own work.

Tell the children that legacy is to be the key word for them in this lesson.

(50 mins) Development
Pose the question – what is history? Write the children's responses (only the positive ones!) on the board or a large sheet of paper. Encourage more able thinkers to identify reasons why it is studied in school.

Look again at the word bank vocabulary. Which of these words and ideas do we use today? Can anyone think of any other things that we have 'inherited' from the Ancient Greeks? Remind them of the research done to date and the ideas in many of the non-fiction texts on display. Record these on a large sheet of paper under the headings: buildings, language, myths and legends, plays and theatres, ways in which to live together.

Point out that another legacy from Ancient Greece was asking questions. Ask children to describe a situation when the questions they asked did not give them the information they needed to know.

CHAPTER 3
ANCIENT GREECE

Why is the
history of
Ancient Greece
important to us?

Learning to ask 'good' questions is a skill. Greek thinkers and philosophers such as Socrates, Plato and Aristotle asked questions to guide their search for knowledge.

Look at a newspaper article. Identify the questions that the reporter must have asked in order to write the story. Children should be able to find examples of *who, when, where, why* and *how* questions. Have them discuss why all these questions must be asked if a news article gives information. Make comparisons with writing a history report.

Give out the newspaper cuttings or photographs with captions, one between two. Ask the pairs to identify how these ask and answer questions.

 Plenary
Ask the children to think about what influence have Greek ideas had on the buildings in their area. Suggest that they need to research into Greek buildings and look at pictures of Greek buildings. Can they find elements of these buildings in the area?

Differentiation
Less able children will need additional support to enable them to understand meanings offered in many glossaries and may need to concentrate on fewer words. Paired work on newspaper photographs should be with a more able child.

More able children could be asked for extended justification for their responses.

Assessing learning outcomes
Can the children define what is meant by the word 'legacy'? Can they give examples of the Greek legacy in everyday life?

How have Greek ideas influenced our buildings?

Background information
Greek architecture was rediscovered by Northern Europeans during their travels to Greece in the 16th and 17th centuries. This produced a rebirth of Greek (and Roman) ideas which led to a fundamental change in the appearance and planning of European buildings.

The Greeks had been able to cut large stones from their marble quarries which could be used as huge beams to support their buildings rather than building arches. By the 5th century they had perfected this beam (lintel) and pillar (post) form of construction. The art of column design became more and more elaborate and columns are the most conspicuous feature of Greek buildings.

Greek architects invented three 'orders' of architecture. These were called the Doric, Ionic and Corinthian. Sometimes a caryatid (the form of a female figure) took the place of an ordinary column.

A circular building was known as a tholos and often used for religious shrines. One of Sir Christopher Wren's earliest works, the Sheldonian Theatre in Oxford, represented this particular adaptation of classical architecture.

What you need and preparation
Obtain photographs of local and regional buildings which demonstrate Greek architecture and display these prior to the lesson with the heading 'Where's the Greek influence?'. Alongside the display, have a large poster of the Parthenon or a similar classical Greek building, pictures from books showing reconstructions of Greek buildings or towns and examples of Greek-inspired architecture, a picture of an Ancient Egyptian temple (if the children have previously studied Ancient Egypt), a photograph of a local building featuring Ancient Greek-style columns (Doric, Ionic or Corinthian), a photograph of the exterior of the British Museum (this can be downloaded from the

CHAPTER 3
ANCIENT GREECE

Why is the history of Ancient Greece important to us?

ICT opportunities
Try an Internet search for 'The Elgin Marbles' – this will find several sites devoted to the campaign for their return to Greece. Encourage children to find out what the Elgin marbles are, where they are kept and why there is a campaign to return them. This can be done as a homework task – either at home, or at school or in the local library.

Follow-up activities
● Let the children research the Parthenon and complete the worksheet on photocopiable page 135 as homework.
● Read about the Elgin marbles and make a case for them staying in the British Museum.

British Museum website) or photographs of Greek-influenced buildings in Edinburgh, and general books on buildings and architecture. Prepare an acetate of photocopiable page 136 and have available an overhead projector. Prepare copies of photocopiable page 135 (one per child). Have available sheets of A4 paper (several per child) and adhesive tape.

What to do

Introduction — 20 mins
Look at the poster of the Parthenon. Ask the children to try to imagine what this would have looked like when it was first built (roof, colours, people using it, and so on). Put particular emphasis on this activity, as children often have a mental image of Greek buildings being derelict. Explain that books and museums often show reconstructions of such buildings to help us imagine them more satisfactorily, and draw their attention to the pictures on display. Point out any friezes on the buildings. Give out copies of photocopiable page 135, and let the children try to reconstruct the Parthenon as it might have looked at the time of the Ancient Greeks. Explain that they can complete it as a homework activity. This provides an opportunity for children to record their understanding of the building as it might have been.

Explain that one of the most distinctive features of Greek buildings was the use of columns. Once Athens became very powerful and wealthy, the rulers spent money on employing architects to create fine buildings. Like today's architects, they borrowed ideas from other cultures. (One area was Ancient Egypt, so if the children have studied this, you could reinforce the links by showing them pictures of Egyptian temple.) The Greek architects invented three 'orders' of architecture. These were called Doric, Ionic and Corinthian. Point out examples in the display.

Development — 50 mins
Show the OHT from photocopiable page 136. Point out the differences between the columns. Look at the photograph of the local building with a Greek architectural influence. Ask children what the building is and what it is used for. Do any of them know how old it is? How has the architect used Greek building designs? Are the columns Doric, Ionic or Corinthian? (It is likely that the columns may be a mixture of styles, but it is only necessary to look for the overall influence.)

Ask the children why architects use columns (for strength). Let the children test this by rolling a sheet of A4 into a cylinder to look like a column, then hold it in place with adhesive tape. Ask them to put the column upright on the floor, then place a book on it so that it balances. Children may need to experiment with the column 'design', so that it can hold the weight.

Look through the resources for other examples of the Greek legacy in architecture. Encourage children to identify other legacies, for example mock-Tudor houses, Victorian Gothic. If the class has studied the Romans, it would be useful for them to look at Roman buildings and decide how the Greeks influenced the Romans. A good understanding of chronology is needed here, so that children are clear who has influenced whom.

Plenary — 20 mins
Show the photograph of the outside of the British Museum and let the children identify the Greek legacy. Tell them that this building was built in the Victorian era, when many architects copied Greek buildings, particularly important public buildings. They would have visited Greece and Rome, and drawn and copied the ancient buildings. Sometimes people would bring back bits of the original buildings. Alternatively, show pictures of Edinburgh and ask children why it has been described as 'the Athens of the North'.

Differentiation
Most of the input in this lesson is visual, so any children with visual impairment will need additional

CHAPTER 3
ANCIENT GREECE

Why is the
history of
Ancient Greece
important to us?

support from the descriptions of other children and through the practical activities of making a column to support a heavy book. Encourage them to feel 'columns' on chair legs, and, if possible, provide some marble for them to touch.

Assessing learning outcomes

Can the children identify the different types of Greek columns? Do they understand that many buildings in our towns today were designed by architects who used ideas from the Greek legacy? Can they identify the Victorian era as a particular time, when public buildings demonstrated Greek architecture? Can they suggest the possible reasons for this?

What stories from Ancient Greece have been handed down?

Background information

There is a distinction between myths and legends. Myths are about powerful and fantastic animals and people who are responsible for creating the world and everything that happens in it. Legends on the other hand start with a grain of truth and then grow into fantastic tales.

The Ancient Greeks believed in a large number of heroes and many of their myths and legends were about these. Heroes were human beings who had superhuman powers which seemed to have come from the gods. The Greeks took it for granted that the gods intervened in the lives of all mortals, but recognised that their presence could be seen particularly in the stories of heroes. Many Greek poems and plays were based on the stories of these heroes.

The most famous of these were poems attributed to the blind Greek poet, Homer. The *Iliad* was an account of an incident during the siege of Tory. The *Odyssey* tells the stories of the wanderings and adventures of another Troyian hero, Odysseus. He spent ten years travelling back from Troy to his island kingdom of Ithaca.

What you need and preparation

Collect reference books, play scripts and stories about the Greek myths. Display books and posters showing examples of Greek mythology in art. Before the session, you need to divide the class into groups and allocate myths for re-enactment. Ensure that they all have a good knowledge of the myth they are to work on and allocate the right number of children for each group, for example Midas (king, god, son, servant); Narcissus and Echo (two people); Theseus and the Minotaur (Theseus, King, Ariadne, servants, Minotaur); Perseus and the Gorgon's head (Perseus, Athene, Andromeda, three Gorgons). Alternatively, you could look at the Odyssey and break it up into separate sections, so that each group takes a section – one child could play the part of Homer, the blind poet, telling his tale and introducing different sections of the story. Provide old sheets for costume-making and props for performance. Have available a board or flip chart and writing materials.

What to do

10 mins Introduction

Remind the children of the work they did in *Who were the Ancient Greeks?*, distinguishing fact from fiction. Point out that sometimes, when events happened a long time ago, there are difficulties in doing this. Myths are the oldest stories and are about powerful, superhuman animals, spirits, gods and goddesses. They have a strong magical element. Legends may start with a grain of truth, which is changed and modified over the years. Archaeologists have long known that some myths, such as the Trojan Wars, are based on fact. If any of the children have been to northern Turkey, they may have been to see the many walls of Troy and the Wooden Horse. Children who have been to Crete may have visited Knossos, where it is believed that earthquakes

Learning objectives
• Have a good knowledge of several Greek myths.
• Consolidate knowledge of differences between myth, legend and biography.
• Develop a concept of heroes and heroines.
• Be able to identify Greek myths in classical paintings.

Lesson organisation
Whole class; groups (size is dependent on the myth being re-enacted), with space for movement; whole class.

Vocabulary
myth
legend
biography

Why is the history of Ancient Greece important to us?

convinced people that there was a dangerous animal (the Minotaur) living under the palace.

Ask the class for examples of any Greek myths they know and record them on the board or flip chart.

Development (50 mins)
Allocate groups to work together on a drama presentation. Allow them access to the retellings of the myths to refresh their memories about the plot if necessary. Provide them with the props and sheeting for making costumes.

Some groups may want to write a script first, others may prefer to discuss and then walk through it. Ensure they recognise the historical aspect of their drama (for example no guns!).

Plenary (30 mins)
Let the groups perform their re-enactments to the rest of the class.

Differentiation
Quieter children need support, but not pressure, to join in with drama. This is particularly important if very little drama is being done in school. Less able children might need help with making costumes.

Assessing learning outcomes
Can the children act out a myth, demonstrating an understanding of it and an awareness of the historical constraints on its presentation? Can they act in role?

(1 hour 30 mins) How has our language been influenced by the Ancient Greeks?

Learning objectives
• Know that many words we use today come directly from the Greeks.
• Know that many more words have prefixes and suffixes which have a Greek origin.
• Identify these words and understand that knowledge of the Greek legacy in language can help in reading and comprehending unfamiliar words.
• Recognise similarities between the Ancient Greek alphabet and the alphabet used today.

Background information
The Greek language is a legacy which permeates our lives. Some words come directly from the Greek – gymnasium, hero, marathon, museum, myth and stadium. Some words originate from a combination of Greek words, such as acrobat which is formed from the two Greek words – *akros* meaning high and *batos*, meaning to walk and hippopotamus from *hippos* (horse) and *potamus* (river). Other words come to our language as prefixes and suffixes, changing or enhancing the meanings of words, for example *bio-* (life), *bi-* (two), *geo-* (earth), *phon-* (sound/voice), *-ology* (study), *-graph* (to write) and *-phobia* (fear). The word alphabet itself comes from Greek *alphabetos* – alpha and beta, the first two Greek letters. Many of the other letters in the English alphabet are directly derived from the Greek.

What you need and preparation
Compile a display of items with Greek names (for example Nike sportswear, Ajax cleaning products). Arrange access to the Internet and a graphics package such as *Word Art*, and have available etymological dictionaries, simple dictionaries, writing materials and a board or flip chart. Prepare copies of photocopiable page 137 for less able children.

What to do
Introduction (30 mins)
Explain that today's session will look at the influence of Ancient Greece on our language. Talk about any children's names with a Greek influence – Helen, Alexander, Jason, Alexandra. Then look at some of the items on display, such as a Nike T-shirt or Ajax scouring powder. Why do the children think that companies have used Greek names? Search on the Internet will show that names such as Aristotle, Socrates and Plato have all been hijacked by different companies and

Why is the history of Ancient Greece important to us?

organisations.

If the children have studied the Romans, Anglo-Saxons or the Vikings, they should be encouraged to link their knowledge of the origin of words with what they have already covered. Talk about other words we use which come from Greek – gymnasium, hero, marathon, museum, myth, stadium and symposium. The word 'history' itself comes from the Greek *historia* (learning from enquiry) and 'drama' from the Greek for to act or to do. Write these words on the board.

Many of the words we use to describe our language come from the Greek – 'alphabet' comes from the first two Greek letters (*alpha* and *beta*), lexicon from *lexis* meaning 'word', 'synonyms' from the Greek words for 'same' and 'name'; 'antonym' from the Greek words for 'opposite' and 'name'.

45 mins **Development**
Let the children use etymological dictionaries to find some words with Greek origins. Ask them to create families of words, using the words on the board as a starting point. Explain to children that they need to start with one word, such as 'gymnasium', look it up and then find other words which are linked to it (gymnastics, gymnast, and so on).

Children could use a graphics package such as *Word Art* to make a display of these words, or alternatively draw a word web of Greek language origins.

15 mins **Plenary**
Share the word family displays. Ask the children if they can think of any additional words which could be in the word families. If some children have been able to make up their own words, establish this as a separate interactive part of the display, which can be added to over time.

Differentiation

Less able children could be given copies of photocopiable page 137 and be asked to find out which letters the Greeks did not have (j, q, v, w and y; c could probably be substituted with k) and then write their own names using the Greek alphabet.

More able children should be asked if they can explain why Greek words have come into our language when the Greeks never settled in the UK. They could also use non-fiction texts to find out prefixes and suffixes with Greek origins such as *bio-, bi, geo-, phon-, tech-, -ology, -graph* and *-phobia*. Sometimes a new word is created from both a prefix and a suffix, for example a technophobe is someone who does not like/fears technology. Can they make up any words themselves?

Assessing learning outcomes

Do the children recognise that some of the words we use have their roots in Ancient Greece? Do they know that letters in our alphabet are very similar to Greek letters? Can they use these to write their own names? Can they identify words with Greek origins in the dictionary and create word families? Are they able to invent new words using Greek roots as a foundation?

Lesson organisation
Whole class; group and paired work; whole class, teacher-led.

Vocabulary
alpha
beta
lexicon
synonym
antonym

ICT opportunities
● *Word Art* or a similar package for could be used for the word family displays.
● Find out if there is a Greek script font or a facility for inserting Greek symbols on the computer, then let children experiment with writing their names in Greek.

Follow-up activity
Find a photograph of a building, statue or frieze where the Greek inscription can be seen clearly. Try to translate it into the English alphabetical system.

1 hour 30 mins ## How have Greek ideas influenced our understanding of citizenship?

Background information

This draws on work already covered in the unit, when children looked at words such as citizen, democracy, monarchy etc. As before it is important to recognise that only a few of the Ancient Greeks were citizens and the notion of citizenship varied from city state to city state. This fits very easily with looking at how citizenship is seen today.

CHAPTER 3
ANCIENT GREECE

Why is the history of Ancient Greece important to us?

Learning objectives
● Consolidate work carried out on Athens as a city state.
● Understand the concept of being a citizen in Athens.
● Be able to define the key characteristics of being a citizen in the UK.
● Be able to compare UK and Ancient Greek ideas of citizenship.

Lesson organisation
Whole class; individual tasks; whole class.

Vocabulary
citizen
polis
city state
democracy
equality

ICT opportunities
Visit the citizenship website. What key information does this give? How useful is it for children in primary schools?

In Ancient Greece there were heavy obligations of citizenship such as having to take part in the assembly which ran the state. Unpopular citizens could be ostracised. All citizens were asked in the sixth month of the year if they wanted an 'ostracism' to be held. If so, it was held at the assembly in the following month. Ostraka were single bits of broken pottery on which the name of the citizen to be ostracised was scratched. It needed 6 000 citizens for an ostracism to be valid. The person then had to go into exile for ten years.

What you need and preparation

Obtain and display a range of non-fiction texts which contain information about citizenship in Athens, together with posters and photographs showing political demonstrations, voting etc. Prepare an enlarged copy of photocopiable page 138 for display and one each for the children. Have available writing materials and a board or flip chart.

What to do

(30 mins) Introduction

Introduce the lesson by asking children for examples of different groups to which they belong (for example family, class, school, faith, football supporters' club, Brownies, Cubs, dance, band). Choose one of these and ask children what it means to be a member. Look at the rules and regulations, rights and duties. How 'democratic' are these (for example does everyone contribute to making the rules in a classroom)? Does being a member of the group mean that you must obey the rules, even if you do not agree?

Point to a photograph of a political demonstration. What happens when people feel very angry about an issue? If possible, give an appropriate local example. What are the problems if someone does break the rules? Talk about how belonging to a particular group makes us a 'citizen' of that group, with both rights and duties. Record this discussion on the board. It is useful to make a note of children who contribute to this debate on the board, so that others are encouraged to follow their example.

An example of the 'rules' for family membership could be being well-behaved and keeping your bedroom tidy, and the 'rights' could include being looked after, having meals cooked, and so on.

(50 mins) Development

Show the class the enlarged copy of photocopiable page 138 and talk through the questions to make sure that the children understand them. Distribute individual copies and ask the children to work through it. Encourage children to use the books on display to find out about citizenship in Ancient Athens to help them answer the questions.

(10 mins) Plenary

Talk about voting and what it entails. When do children vote? When do they see it on television?

Differentiation

Less able children will need additional support during this lesson.

More able children could be allowed to extend their research by increasing the amount of reference texts available.

Assessing learning outcomes

Can children define the vocabulary introduced? Are they able to provide two key features of citizenship in Athens? Can they evaluate the words 'democracy' and 'citizenship' in relation to Ancient Greece and/or the UK today?

The Aztecs

The original History Orders (DES, 1991) incorporated the Aztecs within a much larger compulsory unit entitled Exploration and Encounters. Within this unit, studying the Aztecs reinforced the fact that there were existing civilisations in the 'New World' and provided an example of what happened to many native societies when they were 'discovered'. The 1995 revised history curriculum removed this unit but kept the Aztecs as one of the 'non-European' units. This enabled schools to continue using resources built up when the Aztec period was compulsory.

The suggested key features for the World Study Units in the current Orders (DES, 1999) are:
- the society in relation to other contemporary societies
- chronology; reasons for the rise and fall of the civilisation
- significant places and individuals
- distinctive contribution to history
- aspects of everyday life.

In addition, studying the Aztecs allows investigation into:
- cultural development through recognition of differences and similarities between Aztec culture and Tudor culture or other societies separated in time
- social development through identifying how Aztec society was organised
- moral development through consideration of consequences of actions and events, for example effects on Aztecs of Spanish colonisation (a focus on the Aztecs provides children with a powerful and graphic example of what happens when two cultures clash and when native people came under the rule of European Empires); how different interpretations reflect different viewpoints and values
- citizenship through consideration of exploitation of one society by another; critically evaluating evidence and analysing interpretations of the Aztecs
- use of sources – investigating sources available for a study of the Aztecs offers a valuable opportunity to explore bias and interpretation.

When and where was the Aztec Empire?

The Aztecs were a wandering tribe that settled in the fertile Valley of Mexico. Here they flourished, and by 1519 ruled some 15 million people. The capital of the Aztec Empire, Tenochtitlan, was built in the middle of a huge lake and was linked to the mainland by three bridges/causeways. At the height of the Empire this covered 20 square miles and was larger than the cities of 16th century Europe. The town was divided into four districts, each with its own temples, markets and schools.

The swamp land on which Tenochtitlan was built was reclaimed through an effective system of poles, rush matting and mud. Here they grew a wide range of crops, including squashes, carrots, maize, sweet potatoes and tomatoes. Most Aztecs were farmers and worked with wooden digging sticks as there were no draught animals or ploughs.

Rich Aztecs lived in two-storey homes made from stone or mud brick and with a flat roof. Rooms faced inwards onto a central courtyard. Many families had their own steam bath built near the house. Poorer people lived in one-storey wattle and daub homes with two rooms and a thatched or tiled roof.

The Aztecs believed in many different gods. The sun god was very important to them and required blood to stay alive. Without a regular offering of blood, the sun would disappear, crops would fail and the universe would end. People pricked their ear lobes to offer blood, but most came through human sacrifice of both captives and Aztec people.

Aztecs did not have money, but exchanged goods using a system of barter. All manner of goods were traded in the 24-hour markets which operated every five days in Tenochtitlan. A wide range of goods were sold in different sections of the market and included gold, feathers, animal skins, fruit, vegetables, wild animals, weapons, jewels, pots, herbal medicines, tobacco, slaves and cloaks. Travelling merchants (pochteca) visited the furthest corners of the Aztec Empire to bring back goods to sell.

Aztec art was based on geometric designs and stylised drawings. Craftsmen were important. The main groups were metalworkers who produced fine, highly detailed items of gold, silver and copper. Unfortunately, few of these objects survived the conquest. Featherworkers made beautiful cloaks, headdresses, shields and banners using colourful feathers from exotic birds. Pots were made by hand as the Aztecs did not have the potter's wheel. Colourful textiles were woven on waist looms; similar looms are still used today. The Aztecs did not have the wheel or iron. Their feats of engineering were produced with simple tools.

Hernando Cortes was a Spanish adventurer who entered Tenochtitlan in 1519, accompanied with soldiers and priests. The reception from the Aztecs was initially welcoming, partly because they believed Cortes and his men to be gods. However, the Spanish began to kill the Aztecs to gain the vast amounts of gold the Aztecs possessed. Although the Aztecs were fierce fighters, they did not have the guns, armour, horses or wheeled vehicles that the Spanish had. Moreover, the Spanish had brought with them diseases such as smallpox, to which the Aztecs had no resistance. Consequently by 1521 the Aztec Empire had completely fallen to the Spanish.

UNIT: When and where was the Aztec Empire?

Enquiry questions	Learning objectives	Teaching activities	Learning outcomes	Literacy links	Cross-curricular links
Who were the Aztecs?	• Learn where and when the Aztecs lived. • Learn how and when the Aztecs built up an Empire in Mexico. • Begin to build up a chronology of the Aztec period. • Locate the Aztec period in relation to the Tudor period. • Use information sources to research key events and locate them on a timeline.	Use food items to highlight links between children today and Aztecs. Find out what children know about Empire. Locate Mexico and Mexico City on maps. Establish timeline and locate Aztec move to Mexico. Teacher input on the development of the Aztec Empire. Children complete own map of Mexico and start Aztec timeline. Start Aztec dictionary.	Children: • know where the Aztec Empire was • know that the Aztec Empire was built up over hundreds of years and that it was strongest when the Tudors ruled in England • identify reasons for the rise of the Aztecs in Mexico	Using non-fiction books.	Geography: mapwork. Maths: ordering numbers.
How was the Aztec civilisation organised?	• Learn that Aztec civilisation was organised in different levels. • Devise questions to direct their research into different groups in society. • Use a range of sources to find out about Aztec life.	Ask children to predict what groups of people might have been found in Aztec society. Children arrange these groups in a hierarchy. Use display/labels in pyramid shape to identify the different levels in Aztec society. Use cards to allocate Aztec groups to tables. Allocation of Aztec identity cards within these groupings (age/sex/role). Children research their role/lifestyle.	• identify different groups of people in Aztec society • put these groups in order from the most important to the least important • devise questions about aspects of Aztec daily life • select information from a range of resources to answer these questions	Using non-fiction books (index/contents for example)	Citizenship: diiferent groups in Aztec society. Art: draw Aztec-style pictures.
Who was Cortes and why did he lead an expedition into Aztec territory?	• Learn who Cortes was. • Sequence key events. • Know that that there was more than one reason for the Spanish expedition in Mexico, and put these reasons in order of priority.	Make links to other explorations. Use visual sources and written accounts describing Cortes. Can children suggest what the motives of Cortes might have been? Discuss motives of others involved (soldiers, priests, king of Spain). Use writing frame to explain reasons for the expedition.	• say who lead the Spanish expedition into Aztec land • sort reasons for the expedition into categories • select the most important reasons according to different viewpoints	Using writing frames for explanatory writing.	Geography: mapwork; use of atlas/globe to locate explorations. Moral development: motivation for actions.
How and why did Cortes defeat the Aztecs?	• Know of the sequence of key events in the conquest of the Aztecs. • Be able to apply their understanding of chronology to sequence key events in the conquest. • Understand that they were many reasons for the Aztecs' defeat by the Spanish.	Focus on dates related to Spanish Conquest. Play tape of recreated Pre-Columbian music as background to the story of Montezuma's dream and the arrival of Cortes. Comparison of the two leaders Montezuma and Cortes and their first meeting. Go through key events leading to defeat of Aztecs. Use visual sources to identify differences between Aztec and Spanish armies. Identify reasons for defeat of the Aztecs. Prioritise in order of importance and discuss why chosen. Viewpoints of Aztec warrior and Spanish soldier.	• know the main events leading to the defeat of the Aztecs • identify differences between the Aztec army and Spanish army • understand the reasons for the defeat of the Aztec army by a small Spanish force and identify the most important	Legends	Music: pre-Columbian tape of recreated 'Aztec' music. RE: beliefs of the Aztecs.
What happened to the Aztec Empire?	• Know what happened to the Aztec civilisation. • Understand the effect of the conquest on the Aztec population, Spain and the 'Old World'. • Be able to identify how the conquest can be viewed in different ways. • Be aware that there are traces of Aztec civilisation left today.	Recap on the timeline events. Add Aztec population figures for 1521 and 1568. Children suggest why great decrease. What might have happened? Use written and visual sources to find clues about what happened. Use food examples to explore effects on Europe and Spain. Write from different viewpoints, Aztec and Spanish. Review of tourist brochures, displays of artefacts and visual sources.	• know what happened to the Aztec civilisation • understand how Spain and Europe benefited for the defeat of the Aztecs • are aware of the traces of Aztec civilisation left today and their legacy to modern Mexico.	Using writing frames Expressing points of view	Geography: knowledge of Mexico today. Citizenship: exploitation of Aztec empire. Moral Development: exploration of different points of view.

CHAPTER 4
THE AZTECS

When and where was the Aztec Empire?

Who were the Aztecs?

Learning objectives
● Learn where and when the Aztecs lived.
● Learn how and when the Aztecs built up an Empire in Mexico.
● Begin to build up a chronology of the Aztec period.
● Locate the Aztec period in relation to the Tudor period.
● Use information sources to research key events and locate them on a timeline.

Lesson organisation
Whole class, teacher-led; pairs to investigate Mexico and definition of Empire, then individuals for map and timeline work; whole class.

Vocabulary
Aztec
empire
settlement
tribute
Tenochtitlan

Background information
The Aztecs were originally a wandering tribe who eventually settled in the Valley of Mexico – the only really fertile area of the peninsula. The establishment of the Aztec settlement in the Valley of Mexico was foretold in a dream in which an eagle, sitting on a cactus with a snake in its beak, would mark the place where the Aztecs should build their town. This image appears on the modern Mexican flag. The initial village prospered and Aztec influence grew, mainly through subjugation of neighbouring tribes who had to send a large number of their young men to be sacrificed and pay regular tribute. Inevitably, this caused resentment and motivated other tribes to form alliances with the Spanish against the Aztecs. By 1519, the Aztec Empire ruled 15 million people in 500 towns and cities.

What you need and preparation
Buy or prepare Mexican food items in advance, such as tortillas, tomatoes, cocoa and avocados. Obtain brochures and postcards of Mexico, and a picture of the Mexican flag. Have available a large world map and a range of dictionaries. Prepare individual copies of photocopiable pages 139, 140 and 141 and copy of photocopiable page 139 on acetate. Make a class timeline showing the Tudor monarchs, and prepare cards showing key dates relating to the Aztecs. Have an overhead projector available. Prior to the lesson find out if anyone in the class has ever been to Mexico on holiday.

What to do
③⓪ mins Introduction
Show the children the food items, and ask them to identify them. Does anyone know what country they originated from? Explain that they were introduced to Europe at the time of the Tudors and came from the area known today as Mexico. Locate Mexico on the world map.

Brainstorm what children know about Mexico (from television, holidays, geography work, and so on). If there is little previous knowledge, hand out one resource between two (postcards, tourist brochures, and so on) and allow five minutes for them to look for clues about Mexico. Record their information on the board.

Inform the children that they are going to find out about what was happening in Mexico 500 years ago, at the same time as Henry VIII and Elizabeth I were rulers of England. Establish the timeline (with Tudor monarchs located). Share the key objective with the class – to find out when and where the Aztec Empire existed.

Ask the children if they know what an empire is. Draw on knowledge gained during topic work on the Romans or the Victorians. Get them to look for a definition in their dictionaries.

Use the acetate map from photocopiable page 139 to show the location of other tribes, the movement of Aztecs into the valley of Mexico and their settlement in Tenochtitlan (now modern Mexico City).

Relate the Aztec myth about the location of their capital, then show the modern flag of Mexico to show how the story is commemorated. Give a brief overview of how the Aztec Empire came to be so powerful and introduce Montezuma II. Add relevant dates to the timeline.

④⓪ mins Development
Let children copy the details of the Aztec Empire onto their individual maps of Mexico (photocopiable page 139). They can then enter key dates in the development of the Aztec Empire on their individual timelines (photocopiable page 140).

**ICT
opportunities**
Use timeline
software to print
out an Aztec
timeline and a
separate Tudor
timeline to enlarge
and display next to
each other.

**Follow-up
activities**
● Start a dictionary
of Aztec vocabulary
(writing and
drawing).
● Encourage
researching the
Aztecs at home
(library, Internet or
CD-ROM).

20 mins **Plenary**

Review what has been covered so far. Place the end date of 1568 on the timeline and explain that by this date the Aztec Empire had been defeated and the population had decreased to 2.6 million. Give the children copies of photocopiable page 141 and tell them that it gives key dates in the history of the Aztecs. They will be looking at these events over the course of the next few lessons.

Explain that the next lesson will look at everyday life in Aztec times. Ask children to suggest how they might investigate this and to bring anything they think will be useful.

Differentiation

Pair children of lower and average ability for brainstorming on modern Mexico and the Empire. Offer support for the children when completing timeline and map work.

Children of higher ability could use ICT to look for relevant websites, and conduct research linked to key dates on the timeline to build up key fact cards.

Assessing learning outcomes

Can they find Mexico on a world map? Can they find Tenochtitlan on a map of Aztec Mexico? Can they explain when the Aztec Empire existed? Are the maps and timelines completed correctly?

How was the Aztec civilisation organised?
(1 hour 30 mins)

Background information

Aztec society was hierarchical, with the Emperor at the head and slaves at bottom. By the time of the Spanish conquest, the Emperor usually came from the royal family and ruled with the Snake Woman (a man) as his main advisor. The Emperor was responsible for foreign affairs and war. The Snake Woman controlled city law, taxes and food. Below them came governors of the provinces (Tlatoani), lesser officials (Tecuhtlis), craftsmen and merchants, ordinary people (Maceualtin) and then, at the lowest end of society, the slaves. The higher your class, the closer you lived to the centre of the city. Your position in society affected what clothes, hairstyle and jewels you were permitted to wear. A large number of laws covered all aspects of everyday life and were implemented by a system of courts and judges.

What you need and preparation

Make copies of photocopiable pages 142 and 143 for each child. Provide a wide range of reference books on the Aztecs (for different reading abilities), and CD-ROMs and a computer if possible. Provide the children with scissors, and writing and drawing materials. You will need a board or flipchart.

What to do

20 mins **Introduction**

Recap on the previous lesson, then share the key objective with the children – to use sources and resources to find out about the Aztecs.

Refer back to Tudor England society if this has been studied previously.(Other units studied could also be drawn on.) What do the the children remember about it? What different groups of people were there (for example royalty, nobles, craftsmen, soldiers, peasants)? Who was the most important?

Ask the children to predict what groups of people might comprise Aztec society. Do they think they would be similar social groups?

**Learning
objectives**
● Learn that Aztec
civilisation was
organised in
different levels.
● Devise questions
to direct their
research into
different groups in
society.
● Use a range of
sources to find out
about Aztec life.

**Lesson
organisation**
Whole class;
groups and
individual
research; whole
class.

Vocabulary
hierarchy
merchant
noble
slave

Development

50 mins Give each child a set of labelled pictures from photocopiable page 142. Ask them to cut out and order the pictures from the most important to the least important people in Aztec society. When they have finished, invite individual children to give reasons for their placements.

Allocate groups from Aztec society to groups of children, for example craftsmen, slaves, priests. Include details of age and sex. Then give them each a copy of photocopiable page 143 and talk through the various categories. Explain that they are going to research their roles and make brief notes in the spaces provided. Show the class the resources available and remind them to use contents pages and indexes of books in their research.

Write up any unusual vocabulary the children discover on the board for further discussion.

Finally let the children complete an A4 outline drawing of themselves in their Aztec role for display (for example Jaguar knight, slave, farmer, rich woman).

Plenary

20 mins Talk about any unfamiliar vocabulary identified by the children. Use a couple of examples of the children's role notes to share with the rest of the class. If appropriate, use a hot-seating activity, with children answering questions in role.

Differentiation

Children of lower ability could be provided with a writing frame to focus their research. Identify specific books (or, if necessary, pages) that will provide them with relevant information. The least confident readers can be directed to photographs and illustrations.

Use a wider range of sources for children of higher ability.

Assessing learning outcomes

Can the children order groups correctly? Can they devise questions about daily life? Can they target their research to select relevant information from a range of sources? Do they record information in note form?

Who was Cortes and why did he lead an expedition into Aztec territory?

ICT opportunities
Use CD-ROMs and the Internet as a source of information.

Follow-up activities
● Complete the drawings for a display.
● Continue working on the illustrated Aztec dictionary.

Learning objectives
● Learn who Cortes was.
● Sequence key events.
● Know that that there was more than one reason for the Spanish expedition in Mexico, and put these reasons in order of priority.

Lesson organisation
Whole class; pairs; whole class.

Background information

Hernando Cortes was born in 1485 in Medellin. His family was from the lowest class of the Spanish nobility and their relative poverty probably influenced Cortes to seek his fortune. At the age of 14 he began studying law in Salamanca, but gave this up two years later and went to Seville. In 1504 he reached Hispaniola (Haiti) where he was granted land and slaves. In 1511 he joined a force sent to conquer Cuba and settled there, owning land and mines. In 1518 he was appointed to lead an expedition to the unexplored mainland of Mexico. In 1522, after the defeat of the Aztec Empire, he was made governor-general of New Spain (Mexico) and held the post until 1525. In 1524 one of his captains led a revolt in Honduras and Cortes led the force to put it down. On his return to New Spain in 1526 he found that he had been considered dead and a new governor had been appointed in his place. After unsuccessfully trying to obtain his reinstatement, he returned to Spain where he died unnoticed in 1547.

What you need and preparation

Try to find information on modern examples of exploration (for example space travel, polar expeditions). Find information texts about Cortes and the Conquistadores. Have available some

Vocabulary
exploration
expedition
motives
Christianity
conversion
greed
power
glory

pieces of A4 card and a marker pen. Enlarge photocopiable page 144 for display. Prepare copies of photocopiable page 145 for each child. You will need the acetate map from the first lesson, plus a blank overlay and an overhead projector. Children will also need their copies of their maps and timelines from the first session. Prepare copies of the differentiated writing frames on photocopiable pages 146 and 147 for the children as appropriate. You will need access to a board or flipchart.

What to do

(20 mins) Introduction

Use a modern example of exploration, preferably topical, to get the children to suggest why people go exploring today. Record their ideas on large card labels. Ask whether the cards could be grouped together in any way (for example desire for fame, knowledge).

Make links where appropriate to past explorers they have learnt about (for example Tudor voyagers, Victorian explorers). What other reasons can be added?

Display the enlarged picture of Cortes from photocopiable page 144. Share the key objective with the children – to find out why Cortes led an expedition into the Aztec Empire.

Give out copies of photocopiable page 145 and ask the children what these sources tell them about Cortes. Review what the children have learnt about the Aztecs so far: focus particularly on tribute; possession of gold, silver and precious stones; belief in many gods. Can they then suggest why Cortes would want to lead an expedition into the Aztec Empire? List their ideas on the board.

(50 mins) Development

Use the acetate map from the first lesson and the overlay to plot Cortes' journey from Cuba to Vera Cruz to Tenochtitlan. Invite the children to plot the journey on their own maps from the first lesson.

Talk about the key events in the expedition leading up to the meeting with Montezuma. Ask the children to add these to their own timelines from the first lesson.

Give the children access to the information texts, then ask pairs to find any further clues about Cortes' motives. Add to those already on the board and colour-code them according to what they were (personal, religious, desire for wealth or glory). Discuss which were the most important of these.

Ask who else went with the expedition (soldiers, priests). What motives might they have had?

Let the children use the differentiated writing frames from photocopiable pages 146 and 147 to explain the most important reasons why Cortes led the expedition to Mexico.

(20 mins) Plenary

Review the motives discussed and talk about how they might affect behaviour towards the Aztecs. Emphasise the fact that there was no single reason for the expedition.

Differentiation

Give less able children a set of written and/or pictorial reasons for the expedition, then let them put them in order of importance.

More able children could explore the motivation of Dona Marina (the Indian woman who acted as translator for Cortes). Why did she accompany the Spanish force and act as translator? They could also explore the motives of King Charles V of Spain. Why would he back an expedition?

Assessing learning outcomes

Can the children explain who Cortes was and what he did? Can they sort reasons for the Spanish expedition into categories? Can they select the most important reasons and suggest an order of priority? Do they understand that different individuals had different reasons?

**ICT
opportunities**
Use CD-ROMs
and the Internet to
find information
about Cortes and
Montezuma.

**Follow-up
activities**
● Use the
information found
to produce a
display showing key
individuals (Cortes,
Dona Marina, an
ordinary soldier, a
priest, the King of
Spain) and their
key motives.
● Continue
compiling the Aztec
dictionary.

CHAPTER 4
THE AZTECS

When and where was the Aztec Empire?

 How and why did Cortes defeat the Aztecs?

1 hour 30 mins

Learning objectives
• Know of the sequence of key events in the conquest of the Aztecs.
• Be able to apply their understanding of chronology to sequence key events in the conquest.
• Understand that they were many reasons for the Aztecs' defeat by the Spanish.

Lesson organisation
Whole class; pairs and individuals; whole class.

Vocabulary
conquest
technology
defeat
omen
allies
legend

Background information

The Aztec power rested on the might of the army. All boys trained to be soldiers. The Emperor could draw on 100,000 soldiers, who fought in city groups. The most important warriors were the Jaguar, Eagle and Arrow knights (officers). Each rank had its own regalia. Soldiers could move up through the ranks according to merit. The highest rank was obtained by performing 20 deeds of great bravery. The emphasis was on individual heroism rather than teamwork. Weapons included slings, bows and arrows, clubs and spears. The Aztecs did not have weapons made of iron. Suits of quilted cotton hardened by soaking in salt water and shields provided protection against the enemy. The main purpose of war was to obtain prisoners for sacrifice rather than to fight to the death.

Cortes' expedition consisted of 600 soldiers armed with guns and 16 horses. Spanish soldiers were drilled and organised to work together as a team. They had horses, guns and weapons made of steel. Cortes believed he was doing God's work by taking Christianity to the New World.

The powerful Aztecs were conquered by a much smaller force in a relatively short time. The main reasons for this were:
• Cortes was initially regarded as the returning God Quetzalcoatl and so was welcomed into Tenochtitlan by Montezuma.
• The Aztecs were fatalistic. Recent portents and omens seemed to them to predict a catastrophe.
• Cortes had with him Marina, a Spanish- and Aztec-speaking Amerindian, who translated for and advised him.
• The Spanish army was better organised army and had more effective leadership.
• The Spanish army had better armour and weapons, including guns.
• Horses gave the Spanish force better mobility.
• The Spanish were able to recruit allies from other tribes under Aztec rule.

What you need and preparation

Obtain a cassette of pre-Columbian music and a cassette player, a version of the legend of Quetzalcoatl and his predicted return, and reference books and visual sources showing Aztec warriors and Spanish soldiers. Have on show the class timeline and prepare key event cards to add to it. Make sure the children have access to their individual timelines. Have available pieces of A4 card and a marker pen. Prepare one copy each of photocopiable pages 148 and 150, and one copy per pair of photocopiable page 149.

What to do

20 mins Introduction
Play an excerpt from the tape of recreated pre-Columbian music, and tell or read the legend of Quetzalcoatl. Use the description of the arrival of Cortes to link with the legend. Discuss how this might have influenced how Montezuma reacted to the arrival of the Spanish.

50 mins Development
Use written sources to find out about the meeting between Montezuma and Cortes. Read together the information on photocopiable page 148. Discuss how the legend of Quetzalcoatl had an impact.

Talk about the omens prior to the arrival of the Spanish. Stress the power of these omens, which seemed to predict the arrival of Cortes and the belief that he was a returning god. What did they stop Montezuma from doing? What might he have done if there had been no legend or omens?

Remind the class how, at the time of the meeting between Cortes and Montezuma, the Aztec Empire was powerful and rich. Point out that by 1521 Montezuma was dead, the Aztec Emperor had been captured, and Tenochtitlan destroyed. Ask the children to suggest why they think the Aztecs were defeated in such a short period of time by a small force of Spanish soldiers. Record their ideas on A4 pieces of card.

Talk about the key events in the conquest, adding dates to the timeline as you do so. The children can then add to their individual timelines.

Let the children work in pairs to use visual sources to identify the differences between the Aztec and Spanish armies (armour, weapons), referring to photocopiable page 149. Encourage oral feedback or record the differences in note form. Invite the children to suggest which army would be stronger and why. Talk about the army organisation and leadership.

Put any additional reasons onto pieces of card and add them to the others. As a class, sort the cards with reasons for the defeat of the Aztecs into categories (leadership, army, technology, beliefs). Then give the children copies of photocopiable page 150. Ask them to cut them up and put the reasons in order, according to which they think is most important. Remind them that they must be able to justify their choice.

(20 mins) Plenary

Look at a few examples of the way children have put the reasons for defeat in order of importance. Discuss the results. Does everyone agree? Reinforce the fact that no one reason accounts for the rapid defeat.

Differentiation

Less able children could be asked to list reasons in order, omitting the explanation.

More able children could focus on categorising the reasons and then putting them in order within each category.

Assessing learning outcomes

Can the children recount the sequence of key events in the conquest of the Aztecs? Can they identify a number of reasons for the Aztecs' defeat by the Spanish?

ICT opportunities
Use CD-ROMs and the Internet as a source of information about the Aztecs and Cortes.

Follow-up activity
Continue compiling the Aztec dictionary.

CHAPTER 4
THE AZTECS

When and where was the Aztec Empire?

What happened to the Aztec Empire?

⏱ 1 hour 30 mins

Learning objectives
● Know what happened to the Aztec civilisation.
● Understand the effect of the conquest on the Aztec population, Spain and the 'Old World'.
● Be able to identify how the conquest can be viewed in different ways.
● Be aware that there are traces of Aztec civilisation left today.

Lesson organisation
Whole class; pairs, then whole class review and individual recording; whole class.

Vocabulary
consequence
conquest
conversion
slavery
disease
epidemic
population
trade
technology
power

Background information
The Spanish conquest had a vast impact on the Aztecs and the Old World. The Aztec Empire was destroyed and its land and resources were exploited by Spain. Aztec territory became known as New Spain, and was given to Spanish Conquistadores. Its gold and silver were stolen and sent to the Spanish king (many Aztec artefacts were destroyed or melted down for the precious metals and jewels). Many Aztecs were killed by the Spanish, but also the Aztec population was decimated by 'European' diseases (for example smallpox, measles). However, the Spanish also caught new diseases (for example yellow fever).

There were forced conversions to Christianity and many Aztecs became slaves. Aztec temples were destroyed and many Catholic churches were built. Mexico became a Christian country, with Spanish its main language.

New animals were introduced to Mexico by the Spanish (for example horses, cows, pigs and sheep), and new foods were introduced to Europe (for example maize, tomatoes, potatoes, avocado and cocoa).

What you need and preparation
Obtain examples of food from Mexico, tourist brochures and information on modern Mexico, and a collection of visual and written sources relating to the effects of the conquest. Make copies of photocopiable pages 151 (one between two) and 152 (one each). Have on show the class timeline with labels, and make sure the children have access to their individual timelines. Write the heading 'Consequences' on the board, then underneath divide it into 'Aztecs' and 'Spain and Europe'.

What to do

⏱ 20 mins Introduction
Share the key objective with the children – to discover what happened to the Aztecs as a result of their defeat by the Spanish force.

Recap on the events on the timeline, then add Aztec population figures for 1519 and 1568. Ask the children to brainstorm in pairs to suggest what could have caused a rapid decrease in population. After ten minutes, let pairs feed back their ideas to the whole class. List these on the board in the 'Consequences for the Aztecs' section.

⏱ 50 mins Development
Let the children work in pairs to use written and visual sources to find further clues about what happened to the Aztecs. Give each pair a copy of photocopiable page 151 for reference.

Have a whole-class review of their findings. Note which of their ideas were correct. Clarify these points as consequences for the Aztec people. Add any additional consequences that have been omitted.

Use the samples of food to introduce the effects of the Aztec Empire on Europe and Spain. Talk about other consequences for Spain and Europe. Record these in the 'Consequences for Spain and Europe' section on the board. Choose one example and discuss whether it was a good or bad thing.

Allocate other consequences to pairs of children. Give them five minutes to decide whether they think it was a good or bad consequence and why. Invite feedback from both categories.

Give out individual copies of the preliminary discussion writing frame on photocopiable page 152. Ask them to work through it, giving both the Spanish and Aztec point of view about the conquest.

**When and
where was the
Aztec Empire?**

(20 mins) Plenary
Review what has been learnt about the conquest.

Invite feedback from the children. They can use their preliminary discussion writing frames to put forward viewpoints (Aztec or Spanish) about the conquest. Stress the fact that the conquest had both positive and negative impacts.

Differentiation

Less able children could sort a given list of consequences into good and bad.

Do not give children of higher ability photocopiable page 152, but ask them to produce their own extended list of consequences in three sections (Aztecs, Spain, Europe).

Assessing learning outcomes

Can the children say what happened to the Aztec civilisation? Can they identify some effects of the conquest on the Aztec population, Spain and the 'Old World'? Can they write about the conquest from different points of view? Can they suggest links between the Aztec civilisation and modern Mexico?

**ICT
opportunities**
Use the Internet as a source for tourism information relating to Aztecs and modern Mexico.

**Follow-up
activities**
● Children could look through tourist brochures and information to find an example of the legacy of the Aztecs (for example the Mexican flag, tourism to visit Aztec ruins, museums with collections of artefacts, food, festivals in Mexico).
● Complete the Aztec dictionary.

What sources are available for the Aztecs?

In this unit, children investigate ways in which historians have found out about the Aztecs, including archaeological, visual and written sources. Children find out about the problems associated with some evidence and how this might affect views of the Aztecs.

The unit builds on previous work that children have done with sources, including artefacts and visual, written and oral history. It encourages children to think more critically about how reliable different sources may be. It would follow on from the previous unit in which children have focused on the Empire and its conquest.

To adapt the unit, Year 3 and 4 children could focus on the types of sources and what they tell us about the Aztecs, or concentrate on observation and inference rather than critical evaluation and consideration of bias.

In this unit, children will have opportunities to use words associated with archaeology, for example evidence, excavation, archaeologist; words associated with historical sources, for example primary, secondary, interpretation, point of view, translation, transcription, bias; words associated with the Aztec culture.

Prior learning

It is helpful if the children have:
- some knowledge of the Aztecs in order to make informed judgement about the sources
- worked with a range of historical sources, including artefacts
- had opportunities to view portraits and paintings and know something about why visual sources are produced
- explored purpose and audience when studying different types of written genres
- knowledge of the difference between a primary and secondary source.

UNIT: What sources are available for the Aztecs?

Enquiry questions	Learning objectives	Teaching activities	Learning outcomes	Literacy links	Cross-curricular links
How do we know about the Aztecs?	• Know the range of sources that are available for the Aztecs. • Know the difference between primary and secondary sources. • Begin to understand that each source gives only part of the whole picture. • Understand some of the problems associated with the historical evidence for the Aztecs.	Identify the full range of historical sources that would help people in the future find out about life in England today. List those that are might be available for the Aztecs. In pairs children investigate each type of source find out information about the Aztecs. (Choose examples that focus on different aspects of life.) Review usefulness of historical source types and the gaps in knowledge about the Aztecs.	Children: • identify the range of historical sources • select those sources of information which are available when studying the Aztecs	Discussing artefacts; factual writing.	
What can we find out from artefacts?	• Learn the difference between a replica artefact and a genuine artefact. • Ask and answer questions about the Aztecs using replica artefacts and photographs of artefacts. • Understand why few artefacts survive from Aztec times. • Know that artefacts cannot tell us everything about the Aztecs.	Groups work with replica artefacts. Identify what it is, what it is used for, how it is used. Children suggest what it can tell us about the Aztecs. Discuss use of replicas and reproductions and problems (scale, materials, construction). What might have happened to artefacts produced by the Aztecs? What happened to the Aztec artefacts that did survive (museums, preservation and conservation)? Why have so few survived?	• explain the difference between a replica artefact and a genuine artefact • ask about the Aztecs using replica artefacts and photographs of artefacts • answer questions about the Aztecs using replica artefacts and photographs of artefacts • explain that artefacts cannot tell us everything about the Aztecs	Giving interpretations of artefacts and justifying this.	Geography/maths: using coordinates and grids.
What visual sources are available for Aztec times and how reliable are they?	• Know that there are a range of visual sources which help us find out about the Aztecs. • Know that visual sources were produced by both the Aztecs and the Spanish. • Know that the visual sources for the Aztecs were produced for different reasons and represented different viewpoints.	Identify range of visual sources for the Aztecs. Show examples. List according to whether produced by Aztecs or Spanish. Discuss how might this affect the images in the pictures (purpose? audience?). Use examples showing an important event to consider whether primary or secondary source, reason for production and how this might effect its reliability.	• name some different of the types of visual sources available for the Aztecs • show an awareness that picture sources are produced for different reasons • say how this might influence the reliability of the visual sources		Art: examining sources that convey details of Aztec decorations and style of art. Moral development: viewpoints; bias; interpretation.
What written sources are available for the Aztecs?	• Learn that written sources for the Aztecs were produced for a reason and audience, and reflected the viewpoint of the writer. • Know that the Aztecs had a pictorial writing system. • Understand that most written sources for the Aztecs were produced by the Spanish during or after the conquest.	Arrange for a colleague to come into the classroom and do something dramatic. Ask the children to describe exactly what happened or what the person looked like. Discuss their accuracy and the problems encountered, even though they were all eye-witnesses. Introduce eye-witness accounts as a written source for the Aztec period. Discuss the purpose of these accounts.	• say why eye-witness accounts are not always accurate • identify whether the written sources represent the Aztec or Spanish version of events • suggest some of the problems presented by written sources for the Aztecs	Describing event or person (speaking and listening); purpose of audience for written accounts.	Citizenship: evaluating sources; exploring interpretation. Moral development: bias; point of view; reasons for actions.
What secondary sources are available and how were they created?	• Know the range of historical interpretations available when learning about the Aztecs. • Understand how historical interpretations are created. • Know that a good historical interpretation is based on primary sources. • Be able to compare different interpretations. • Understand that they can create their own interpretation of Aztec life.	Revise range of primary sources and suggest secondary sources available for studying the Aztecs. Discuss how these are produced. Compare illustrations in books. Identify similarities and differences in the interpretations. Children allocated one interpretation which provides information about a particular aspect of Aztec life. Children draw own interpretation and then compare. Discuss differences, similarities and reasons for these.	• say what types of interpretations are available when learning about the Aztecs • describe how an interpretation is made • explain the features of a good interpretation of history.	Exploring different ways of communicating information; discussing and explaining interpretations.	Citizenship: evaluating/analysing interpretations Moral development: bias; point of view.

**CHAPTER 4
THE AZTECS**

What sources are
available for the
Aztecs?

How do we know about the Aztecs?
1 hour 30 mins

**Learning
objectives**
● Know the range
of sources that are
available for the
Aztecs.
● Know the
difference between
primary and
secondary sources.
● Begin to
understand that
each source gives
only part of the
whole picture.
● Understand some
of the problems
associated with the
historical evidence
for the Aztecs.

**Lesson
organisation**
Whole class, then
pairs for
brainstorming;
pairs for work on
sources; whole
class.

Vocabulary
evidence
artefact
archaeology
archaeologist
historian
excavation
ruins
site
visual source
written source
primary source
secondary source

Background information
The main available sources for finding out about the Aztecs are as follows.
● Buildings – Mexico City (one of the largest cities in the world) now occupies the former site of Tenochtitlan. The ruins of Aztec temples have also been found outside the city.
● Artefacts – excavation has unearthed domestic items, but few of the artefacts made from precious metals have survived.
● Visual material – this includes the Codices, which were Aztec books using pictograms showing aspects of Aztec life (later versions were commissioned by the Spanish) – and paintings produced by Spanish artists at the time and over the following two centuries. There are also modern paintings of Aztec life produced by Mexican artists.
● Written material – the Aztecs did not have a traditional system of writing, but used a system based on pictograms and ideograms. All written evidence comes from Spanish scribes and translators. Aztec poems and stories were written down by Catholic priests after the conquest. There are also eye-witness accounts from Cortes, his commanders, soldiers, and priests.

What you need and preparation
Assemble a collection of Aztec sources (photographs of artefacts and ruined buildings, visual sources, written sources). The sources should focus on different aspects of Aztec life. Display each type of source on a separate table. Ideally you should have several copies of each source so that more than one pair can work at the table. Make large labels for each source table (artefacts, sites, visual, written). Make copies of photocopiable pages 153 (one between two) and 154 (one per child). Have available a board with a range of coloured chalks or pens.

What to do

20 mins Introduction
Share the key objective with the class – to find out how we know about the Aztec civilisation and their way of life.
Ask the children to work in pairs and brainstorm a list of the historical sources that would help people living 100 years in the future find out about life in Britain today. Invite pairs to offer ideas and write these on the board.
Use coloured chalks or pens to colour-code sources according to whether they are primary (from the time) or secondary (produced later). Invite children out to cross out those sources which would not be available for the Aztecs who lived 500 years ago (for example photographs, archive film, video). Children can then list individually the type of sources available for the Aztecs.

50 mins Development
Recap on the main type of sources available for the Aztecs – the main sources of information for historians interested in this civilisation.
Tell the children that they are going to work as history detectives looking at the evidence available about the Aztecs. Ask them to work in pairs and move round from table to table to investigate each source in turn. They should then complete photocopiable page 153 to identify what the sources tell them about the Aztec civilisation and to begin to evaluate the usefulness of each type of source.

20 mins Plenary
Discuss each type of source in turn. What information does it provide about Aztec life? Compare responses from the children to identify any differences in interpretation about a particular

CHAPTER 4
THE AZTECS

What sources are
available for the
Aztecs?

source. Why might there be such differences? What problems does each type of source present? Which source is most useful? Why? Are there any aspects of Aztec life that are not represented by the sources or evidence?

Distribute copies of photocopiable page 154 and tell the children that these are going to be part of an ongoing fact file that they can complete as they acquire information about the Aztecs to build up a class resource.

Differentiation

Provide adult support for less able children when working with written source material.

Ask more able children to prioritise the sources in order of usefulness and give their reasons.

Assessing learning outcomes

Can children say which sources would be available for the Aztecs? Can they say which sources would not be available? Can they say which is a primary source or a secondary source? Can they suggest some of the problems associated with the different types of sources available for the Aztecs?

ICT opportunities
Use CD-ROMs and museum websites to access photographs of Aztec artefacts and ruins.

 # What can we find out from artefacts?

Background information

There are few surviving artefacts left for this period. Although genuine artefacts can only generally be seen in museums, replica Aztec artefacts can be obtained from educational catalogues and specialist mail order companies who deal in resources for history, for example History in Evidence, Articles of Antiquity, Mexicolore. Replicas offer children a chance to observe using the senses. Care must be taken that they do not get incorrect information about materials, construction, scale. It is important that the teacher explains what a replica is.

What you need and preparation

Obtain photographs of excavated sites in Mexico, replica artefacts and photographs of the originals. One of the artefacts should be a broken fragment. Display the replicas and photographs on a table, and give each a number. Draw a grid with coordinates on a large sheet of paper. Make numbered cards, corresponding to the numbers of the artefacts. You will also need Blu-Tack and a copy of photocopiable page 155 for each child. You will need access to the board or flip chart.

What to do

20 mins **Introduction**
Talk about the role of archaeology in learning about the Aztecs. Show photographs of excavated sites in Mexico City. Remind them that this is the site of the Aztec capital, Tenochtitlan. You could possibly relate this to other units studied such as Ancient Egypt and Ancient Greece.

Explain how archaeologists mark out sites with string to produce a grid and that each find is recorded (drawn) and its location noted on paper using coordinates relating to the string grid. Show the large grid and draw attention to the coordinates.

Show the class the piece of broken replica, and encourage them to suggest some of the difficulties archaeologists face. Ask them to suggest what areas of Aztec daily life artefacts

Learning objectives
● Learn the difference between a replica artefact and a genuine artefact.
● Ask and answer questions about the Aztecs using replica artefacts and photographs of artefacts.
● Understand why few artefacts survive from Aztec times.
● Know that artefacts cannot tell us everything about the Aztecs.

Lesson organisation
Whole class; pairs for investigation of replica artefacts; whole class.

What sources are available for the Aztecs?

Vocabulary
artefact
replica
archaeology
archaeologist
excavation
site
find
scale

might help us investigate. List these on the board.

Explain that the class is going to carry out a mock excavation in Mexico City. The task will involve investigating a number of replica artefacts and photographs of artefacts. Use Blu-Tack to stick numbers on the grid to represent where the replica Aztec artefacts were found.

40 mins Development
Let the children work in pairs to investigate and discuss three of the replicas and/or photographs. Give them copies of photocopiable page 155 where they can draw simple sketches, and note their ideas.

30 mins Plenary
Compare the interpretations for each replica and photograph, and invite the children to explain how they came to their conclusions. Identify all the artefacts, what they were used for, how they were used, and what they tell us about the Aztecs. As a class, sort the replicas and pictures into categories relating to the aspect of Aztec life for which they provide information (for example personal decoration, religious ceremonies, leisure). What aspects of life are not represented? Why might that be? What other sources could we look at? Can the children suggest why there are relatively few artefacts left from the Aztec period (destroyed, worn out, lost)?

Talk about how many Aztec artefacts were taken by the Spanish, melted down and shipped to Spain as bullion. Discuss the role of museums in preserving those that are left. Discuss the use of replicas and reproductions, and the problems associated with them (scale, availability of materials, methods of construction).

Differentiation
Less able children should work with the replicas rather than photographs.

More able children could use reference books to find out about the destruction of Aztec artefacts made from precious metals and their transportation to Spain.

Assessing learning outcomes
Can the children explain the difference between a replica artefact and a genuine artefact? Can they ask and answer questions about the Aztecs using replica artefacts and photographs of artefacts? Do they understand that artefacts cannot tell us everything about the Aztecs? Can they say why many Aztec artefacts have not survived?

ICT opportunities
Look at websites for museums holding Aztec artefacts in their collections.

Follow-up activities
• Create museum cards for each replica artefact and add them to the display.
• Continue with work on the fact file.

1 hour 30 mins What visual sources are available for Aztec times and how reliable are they?

Learning objectives
• Know that there is a range of visual sources which help us find out about the Aztecs.
• Know that visual sources were produced by both the Aztecs and the Spanish.

Background information
Visual sources for the Aztec period include the Codices, which were Aztec paper-bark folding books using pictograms and ideograms. These were produced by professional scribes and show aspects of Aztec life and important events. Most of these books were burnt by the Spanish during the conquest or at a later date by Catholic priests. There are also picture accounts produced by other tribes who helped Cortes. For example the *Lienzo de Tlaxacala* (canvas of Tlaxcala) was a painting on a long roll showing key events. This was produced by the Tlaxcallans, allies of Cortes, and was presented to Charles V of Spain. Surviving examples of these books take the traditional book form and were drawn by native artists under commission from the Spanish who wished to record the history and culture of the Aztec people. Thus the Aztec version of their history was in fact recorded by the Spanish. One of the most famous is the *Codex Mendoza* (1541), a pictorial

**CHAPTER 4
THE AZTECS**

What sources are
available for the
Aztecs?

account of Aztec life commissioned by Viceroy Don Antonio Mendoza in order to record the Aztec culture. Native artists produced the Codex incorporating material from some of the older examples.

Paintings were produced by Spanish artists to record dramatic and significant events, for example the capture of Tenochtitlan. Examples were produced at the time and over the following two centuries, all glorifying the Spanish conquests.

There are also modern paintings produced by Mexican artists, celebrating the pre-Colombian Amerindian culture.

The reason for producing a visual source can have a powerful impact on how accurately an event or person is recorded. Aztec Codices were produce to record daily life; Spanish paintings and portraits reflected the need to present a powerful image.

What you need and preparation
Collect together a range of visual sources for the Aztecs (including extracts from the Codices, Spanish paintings, photographs of carvings, portraits of Cortes or Montezuma, and illustrations from non-fiction books). Prepare copies of photocopiable pages 156 and 157.

What to do
(30 mins) Introduction
Recap on what the children have learnt about artefacts. Introduce the focus for the lesson – the use of visual or picture sources. Remind the children of the difference between primary sources and secondary sources, and refer to examples. Identify the range of visual sources available for the Aztecs (picture books or Codices, paintings, portraits, carvings). Explain who produced the sources and how the visual examples reflect one person's interpretation of events (for example the Spanish artist or the Aztec scribe).

Look at each source in turn and discuss whether they were produced by the Aztecs or the Spanish. Discuss how this might affect the content of the pictures. Pick a few examples and talk about whether they are primary or secondary sources, who produced them, the intended audience, the reason for production and how this might affect reliability.

Let the children work individually to complete photocopiable page 156.

(40 mins) Development
Let the children work in pairs to look at photocopiable page 157 and to compare images of the same aspect produced by an Aztec artist and a Spanish painter. Encourage them to look for differences in how people and actions are represented.

(20 mins) Plenary
Invite feedback on the differences they found in the two versions of the event. Discuss whether one version is more reliable and why.

Differentiation
Less able children may need adult support when working with photocopiable page 156.

More able children could look in reference books for other examples of visual sources showing the same event or person from the Aztec period, then compare the versions.

Assessing learning outcomes
Can children list the range of visual sources which help us find out about the Aztecs? Can they identify visual sources that were produced by the Aztecs or the Spanish? Can they identify some of the reasons for the production of visual sources? Can they explain why this might influence the way people and events are represented?

**• Know that the visual sources for the Aztecs were produced for different reasons and represented different viewpoints.
• Understand that visual sources are not always accurate.**

Lesson organisation
Whole class and individuals; pairs; whole class.

Vocabulary
Codex
carving
painting
portrait
illustration
artist
scribe
commission
point of view

ICT opportunities
Look at museum websites to provide access to visual sources for the Aztecs.

Follow-up activity
Get the children to work individually to produce a page for a class Codex showing the daily life of the Aztecs. Allocate different areas of life to the children to ensure wide coverage. Let them use reference books and examples to help them draw in the same style.

CHAPTER 4
THE AZTECS

What sources are available for the Aztecs?

 # What written sources are available for the Aztecs?

Learning objectives
• Learn that written sources for the Aztecs were produced for a reason and audience, and reflected the viewpoint of the writer.
• Know that the Aztecs had a pictorial writing system.
• Understand that most written sources for the Aztecs were produced by the Spanish during or after the conquest.
• Know what a translation is.
• Know that eye-witness accounts are not always accurate.

Lesson organisation
Whole class; pairs and individuals; whole class.

Vocabulary
eye-witness
diary
account
bias
translator
translation
transcribe
transcription
scribe

Background information
The Aztecs did not have a traditional system of writing, but used a system based on pictograms and ideograms. All the available written evidence comes from Spanish scribes and translators. All eye-witness accounts therefore come from the Spanish point of view and were written after the events took place.

There are several translations of Aztec poems and stories which were written down by Catholic priests after the conquest. A particularly beautiful example is called 'The Broken Spears' and children will be working on extracts from this poem during the activity.

There are also numerous eye-witness accounts. Bernard Diaz was a companion of Cortes who wrote his eye-witness memoirs at the age of 70. Other Conquistadores who travelled with Cortes also recorded their memories, such as Tapia and Aguilar. Some of these accounts do show a level of sensitivity towards the native population. Cortes himself provided an account of his expedition in his letters to Charles V of Spain.

What you need and preparation
Brief a colleague or other adult to enter your classroom and either do something particularly dramatic or spend a few minutes talking to you. Prepare copies of photocopiable pages 158, 159 and 160 for each child.

What to do
30 mins Introduction
Recap on the sources and evidence covered so far. Explain that the focus today will be on written evidence and sources.

Then let children witness the pre-arranged event with the visitor to the classroom. When the person has left, ask the children to describe exactly what happened or (if the visitor is unknown to them) what the person looked like. Discuss their accuracy and the problems encountered when trying to remember exactly what happened, even though they were all eye-witnesses to the same event.

Ask the children to describe a shared event in school from the previous month or term. Could they describe the sequence of events, what people did, and what everyone was wearing on that occasion? What did they feel like at the time? Discuss the difficulties of remembering accurately and what we might do if we had to fill in the gaps to provide a full account of the occasion.

Introduce eye-witness accounts of events relating to the Aztecs as a type of written source. Identify which people produced these written 'eye-witness' accounts (Cortes, soldiers, priests). Discuss the motives of the writer, the purpose for writing, when the piece was written, who was the intended audience, and the bias and point of view for each category of eye-witness.

Explain that there are few written sources giving the Aztecs' version of events. The Aztecs only had a picture writing system which was limited in what it could describe. The main available written sources from Aztecs were transcribed by Spanish priests.

40 mins Development
Ask the children to read through photocopiable pages 158 and 159, which give examples of written sources. Ask them to identify which piece of writing is written from an Aztec or Spanish viewpoint and give reasons. Give them copies of photocopiable page 160 to fill in. (Answers: 1. Aztec (Broken Spears); 2. Spanish soldier; 3. Aztec (Broken Spears); 4. Aztec (version as told to Spanish priest.)

CHAPTER 4
THE AZTECS

What sources are
available for the
Aztecs?

 Plenary

20 mins Let the children feed back their ideas for each of the written examples. Consider the problems involved in reliability. Discuss how they could check the accuracy (compare with other related historical sources).

Differentiation

Provide adult support for less able children.

More able children could be asked to find further examples of written eye-witness accounts in reference books and identify whose point of view they are written from.

Assessing learning outcomes

Can the children say why eye-witness accounts are not always accurate? Can they identify whether the written sources represent the Aztec or Spanish version of events? Can they suggest some of the problems presented by written sources for the Aztecs?

Follow-up activity
Continue work on the Aztec fact file.

What secondary sources are available and how were they created?

(1 hour 30 mins)

Background information

It is likely that the children will make extensive use of secondary sources when studying the Aztecs. The main secondary visual sources are illustrations in non-fiction books, recreated scenes from Aztec life acted out as part of a television programme, film or video, graphics in software and CD-ROMs, and museum reconstructions. Secondary written sources included non-fiction texts and historical fiction. It is important that children begin to understand how secondary sources are produced, and what constitutes a useful secondary source. Non-fiction books on the Aztecs generally include illustrations of the same aspects of Aztec life and these can provide an accessible way of encouraging children to compare images. In some instances, details are absent or conflicting. On occasion, books include examples of the primary source material that provided the basis of their illustrations. Looking at different types of visual secondary sources helps children understand the process of their production and that good accurate secondary sources are those based on research and primary evidence. The children can put this into practice when producing their own visual sources about Aztec life, based on differing secondary source material.

What you need and preparation

Make colour copies of two illustrations from different books showing the same aspect of Aztec life (for example farming, fishing, warriors), so that the children can have one set between two. Assemble a range of interpretations which focus on one feature of Aztec life (for example temple, market, home of rich Aztecs). These could include a video excerpt, a photograph of a reconstructed scene in a museum, a computer program, book illustrations, a recording of a radio programme and so on. Ensure AV equipment is available and working (TV, cassette player, computer).

What to do

20 mins **Introduction**

Recap on the range of primary sources available for studying the Aztecs and what the children have learnt over previous lessons. Explain that the focus for today's lesson is on secondary sources for the Aztecs and historical interpretation.

Ask the children to suggest different types of secondary sources. List these on the board (video, museum reconstruction, CD-ROM image, website image, book illustration, etc). Explain

Learning objectives
● Know the range of historical interpretations available when learning about the Aztecs.
● Understand how historical interpretations are created.
● Know that a good historical interpretation is based on primary sources.
● Be able to compare different interpretations.
● Understand that they can create their own interpretation of Aztec life.

Lesson organisation
Whole class; pairs, groups and individuals; whole class.

**CHAPTER 4
THE AZTECS**

What sources are
available for the
Aztecs?

that these are secondary interpretations (they have been produced by people who did not witness the events).

Ask the children to suggest how secondary sources are produced. For example, if a team is producing a television series on the Aztecs for school children, how do they decide what information to put in the programmes? How do they ensure that the reconstructions in the film are accurate? Emphasise the need for a good secondary interpretation to be based on other source material (usually primary sources).

Let the children work in pairs to compare the two illustrations from different books showing the same aspect of life. Encourage them to identify similarities and differences in the interpretations.

50 mins **Development**
Explain to the children that they are going to work in groups to investigate one aspect of Aztec life. Each group will be allocated one type of interpretation and they are to use this to create their own interpretation. Allocate secondary interpretations to each group (for example video extract, photograph of museum reconstruction, CD-ROM illustration, book illustration) on a particular aspect of Aztec life, for example Aztec markets, homes, temples.

Explain that they have to look carefully and then draw their own interpretation based on the information they get from the secondary source allocated to them.

20 mins **Plenary**
Show examples from each group and compare the results. Discuss the differences and similarities between interpretations. Ask the children to suggest reasons for the differences.

Review the range of sources and interpretations investigated during the Aztec topic. Discuss the advantages and problems they have identified during the lessons. What have the children learnt about investigating a time in the past, such as the Aztecs?

Differentiation
Do not allocate the cassette extract to less able children. No other differentiation is needed for this activity.

ICT opportunities
Use video extracts, CD-ROMs and the Internet as source of information.

Assessing learning outcomes
Can the children say how historical interpretations are created? Can they explain that a good historical interpretation is based on primary sources? Can they identify similarities and differences between two interpretations?

THE VICTORIANS: Children in Victorian Britain
What was life like for Victorian children? Page 12

PHOTOCOPIABLE

Images of childhood

What does each source tell us about life for children in the Victorian period? Does each source give us an attractive picture of childhood?

Source 1

© PHILIP SAUVAIN

Source 2

Girl crossing-sweeper
The child had a peculiarly flat face, with a button of a nose. When she spoke there was not the slightest expression visible in her features: indeed one might have fancied she wore a mask and was talking behind it; but her eyes were shining the while as brightly as those of a person in a fever. The green frock she wore… was turning into a kind of mouldy tint: also she wore a black stuff apron, stained with big patches of gruel, "from feeding baby at home" as she said. "I'm twelve years old please, sir, and my name is Margaret R and I sweep the crossing…Mother's been dead these two year, sir, and father's a working cutler, sir; and I lives with him, but he don't get much to do and so I'm obligated to help him. Since mother's been dead, I've had to mind my little brother and sister…father depends on me to look after them…I takes them with me when I go crossing sweeping and they sits on the steps close by. Sister's three and a half year old and brother's five year. So he's just beginning to help me, sir."

Young Mike's statement
Mike… was a short, stout set youth, with a face like an old man's for his features were hard and defined, and the hollows had got filled up with dirt till his countenance was brown as old wood carving. I have seldom seen a boy so dirty. Mike wore no shoes, but his feet were as black as if cased in gloves with short fingers. His coat had been a man's and the tails reached his ankles: one of the sleeves was wanting and a dirty rag had been wound around the arm in its stead. His hair spread about like a tuft of grass where a rabbit had been squatting.

Taken from Spring Books London edition of 'Mayhew's London' first published 1851

Why are these two sources from the Victorian times so different?

PHOTOCOPIABLE

THE VICTORIANS: **Children in Victorian Britain**
What was life like for Victorian children in rich or middle class homes? Page 14

Name _____ Date _____

Victorian children

Question _____

Rich children	Middle class children

PHOTOCOPIABLE

Mayhew's London

Read these accounts and answer the questions.

Account 1

from *Mayhew's London* – The girl crossing-sweeper
"I'll be fourteen, sir, a fortnight before next Christmas…Father came from Ireland and was a bricklayer…He's dead now – been dead a long time sir. I wasn't above 11 at that time. About 12 month after father's death, mother was taken bad with the cholera, and died. I then went along with both grandparents until I got a place as a servant of all work. I was only just above eleven then sir. I hadn't to do any work, only just clean the rooms and nuss [nurse] the child. After grandfather died, grandmother said she couldn't keep me, and so I went out begging – she sent me. I carried lucifer matches… I suppose I used to make sixpence a day and I used to take it home to grandmother, who kept and fed me."

● Why do you think the girl had to work?
● What dangers did the girl face in her life?

Account 2

The Farm Labourer's Home – a letter in the *Morning Chronicle* (1849–51)
You approach the doorway through the mud…You have to stoop for admission…There are but two rooms in the house – one below and the other above. On leaving the bright light without, the room in which you enter is so dark that for a time you can only with difficulty discern the objects which it contains…What could be more cheerless or comfortless? Yet you fancy you could put up with everything but the close earthy smell, which you endeavour in vain to escape by breathing short and quickly.

As you enter, a woman rises and salutes you timidly. She is not so old as she looks, for she is careworn and sickly. She has an infant in her arms, and three other children, two girls and a boy, are rolling along the damp uneven brick floor at her feet. They have nothing on their feet, being clad only down to the knees in similar garments of rag and patchwork. They are filthy, and on remarking it, we are told whiningly by the mother that she cannot keep them clean. By and by, another child enters, a girl, with a few pieces of dry wood, which she has picked up in the neighbourhood for fuel. Nor is this the whole family yet. There are two boys who are out with their father at work…

The eldest girl holds the child, whilst the mother takes a pot from the fire, and pours out of it into a large dish a quantity of potatoes. This together with a little bread and some salt butter for the father and the two eldest boys, forms the entire repast. There is neither beef, bacon, nor beer. Bread, potatoes and water form the dinner…They had a little bacon on Sunday last – it is now Thursday – and they will not taste bacon till Sunday again.

● How many children are there in this family?
● Consider the accommodation. What would it have been like to live and sleep in this cottage?

PHOTOCOPIABLE

THE VICTORIANS: Children in Victorian Britain
What sort of work did Victorian children do? Page 17

Working children – 1

Letter to the Morning Chronicle (1849-51) about Birmingham Factory Women and their Families

My mother had eleven children, of whom I was the eldest. She was employed in the button manufacture all that time… It was my business, as the eldest child, to nurse the younger ones. I was a nurse at five years old, and had sometimes to mind the children at home that they did not set their pinafores on fire… I was put to work at the buttons at seven years of age, and I thought myself very fortunate in being relieved from my disagreeable labour of nursing the baby.

Children's Employment Commission (1864)

A girl speaking to the commission about glove making said that her 5 and a half year old sister, after two years experience, could stitch very well. She continued. 'Little children are kept up shamefully late, if there is work, especially on Thursday and Friday nights, when it is often till 11 or 12… Mothers will pin them to their knee to keep them to their work, and, if they are sleepy, give them a slap on the head to keep them awake. If the children are pinned up so, they cannot fall when they are slapped or when they go to sleep… The child has so many fingers set for it to stitch before it goes to bed, and must do them.'

PHOTOCOPIABLE

Working children – 2

Agricultural labourer's boy

When I am at not at work I do not often get bread and meat for dinner… I had rather work than play, you get most victuals when you work.

A cutler's apprentice

My father was under 12 years of age when he left the Charity School. He was bound to the Cutler's Hall to a Mr Edward Windle… who carried on a business as a manufacturer of table knives: an austere and severe master… As the youngest boy he

becomes the slave to all above him… He has to learn his trade… the master leaves his instruction to the elder 'prentices and they cuff him and beat him because he cannot by intuition do as well as themselves: for every job too he is taken from his work. He has to mend the fire, clean the workshop and do all other things pertaining to the trade… he must clean the knives, grease and black his master's, his mistress's and the children's shoes, as well as those of the elder 'prentices… Their dinner was sent out for them into the kitchen and everyone helped himself, the eldest of course taking the lion's share and leaving but little for the poor young boy…

PHOTOCOPIABLE

THE VICTORIANS: **Children in Victorian Britain**
What sort of work did Victorian children do? Page 17

Name _____ Date _____

Victorian child worker profile

Name _____

Age _____

Family _____

Occupation _____

Hours worked each day _____

Wage per day _____

Work done in one day _____

_____

_____

Best part of job _____

_____

_____

Worst part of job _____

_____

_____

Reason for working _____

_____

_____

Extract from St Anne's Infant School Log Book

The Curriculum (from HMI Report)
First Class (32 infants six to seven)
'They read Irish Board Books and Catholic Primers, 27 wrote on slates from dictation, short words and single letters. They worked on sums in addition and subtraction. The girls learned to hen and seam.'

Second class (30 children under six)
'Read from cards and a little from the Irish book. They were beginning to write short words, could form figures pretty well and repeat their multiplication tables up to four times.'

Two younger classes were on the gallery (from two years of age)
'The Mistress took this class. They were learning to spell and were daily taught the elements of writing and can work on simple problems with the aid of the Arithmeticon.'

1865
The Mistress examined all classes and found 'January 19th…deficient in subtraction, not being able to do it quickly.'

Topic lessons 1882
Dec and Jan 1882
Animals: the Cat, lion, leopard. Comparison of the above.
Objects – Cottons, silk, wool, leather, glass.
Geography – Divisions of Land and Water. A river, a lake. Winter.
Kindergarten – Drawing on slates.

1899
May 'Pen and pencil drill and also one for passing of slates given to teachers.'

1902
Dec. 'Slight change in the timetable for the time being to allow for drill sergeant giving a course of lessons.'

Punishment
1900
May 'Hints given to the assistants on some points of the 'New Instructions', special stress being laid upon the administering of corporal punishment.'

Pupil sickness and problems
1865
October 13th 'James Rutherford, 4 years old, died. He had 223 attendances.'

1872
Nov 24th 'The teachers went on Monday to enquire after absent children. Two have died but many of the others are doing well.'

1866
October 1st 'Peter Murphy, a child of five years is taken to the workhouse having been abandoned by both father and mother.'

PHOTOCOPIABLE

Name _____ Date _____

Victorian education worksheet

Questions

1. Name some of the schools to be found in 1850 in Victorian Britain.

_____

2. How were the richer children educated?

_____

3. Why were the poor children not receiving education?

_____

4. What major Act of Parliament altered education provision for the poor and when was it passed?

_____

5. What did this Act of Parliament provide?

_____

6. By the end of the Victorian period, in what ways was school different from now?

_____

_____

7. Choose one of the types of school and find out more about it.

_____

_____

_____

Name _____   Date _____

Texts for copying

Cleanliness is next to Godliness.

_____

_____

_____

_____

Spare the rod and spoil the child.

_____

_____

_____

_____

The capital of Great Britain is London.

_____

_____

_____

_____

Queen Elizabeth was the daughter of Henry the Eighth.

_____

_____

_____

_____

THE VICTORIANS: **Victorian towns and town life**
How did towns develop during the Victorian period? Page 25
PHOTOCOPIABLE

Name _____   Date _____

Using commercial directories to chart changes

1. Look at the oldest directory extract. Find out what the population of the town was then. Record this on the chart below in the first box.

2. Look then at the lists of butchers, public houses (or inns) and schools. Count the numbers and record the total in the box. Record the types of other shops or businesses listed.

3. Repeat this task for the next two directory entries, recording your findings in the correct box.

4. Answer the question at the end.

	Population	**Butchers, pubs and schools**	**Other businesses**
Extract 1			
Extract 2			
Extract 3			

In what ways did the town change during the Victorian period?

Name _____   Date _____

Looking at maps

| **Map 1** | **Map 2** | **Map 3** |

● Choose a small area that has changed over the years.

● Copy the changes shown on the maps into the boxes.

In what ways did the town expand in the Victorian period?

_____

_____

_____

_____

_____

_____

PHOTOCOPIABLE

THE VICTORIANS: Victorian towns and town life
What were the housing and pub;lic health problems during the Victorian period? Page 27

Poor housing – 1

[Two men hear that a fellow worker, Davenport, is sick. They visit his home to see if they can help the family.]

On the way Wilson said Davenport was a good fellow,… that his children were too young to work but not too young to be cold and hungry; that they had sunk lower and lower, and pawned thing after thing, and that now they lived in a cellar in Berry Street, off Shore Street…Our friends were not dainty, but even they picked their way till they got to some steps leading down into a small area, where a person standing would have his head about one foot below the level of the street, and might at the same time, without the least motion of his body, touch the window of the cellar and the damp muddy wall right opposite. You went down one step even from the foul area into the cellar in which a family of human beings lived. It was very dark inside. The window-panes of many of them were broken and stuffed with rags, which was reason enough for the dusky light that pervaded the place even at mid-day…the smell was so foetid as almost to knock the two men down. Quickly recovering themselves, as those inured to such things do, they began to penetrate the thick darkness of the place, and to see three or four little children rolling on the damp, nay wet, brick floor, through which the stagnant, filthy moisture of the street oozed up: the fire-place was empty and black; the wife sat on her husband's lair and cried in the dank loneliness…In the dim light, which was darkness to strangers they (the children) clustered around Barton and tore from him the food he had brought with him. It was a large hunk of bread but it had vanished in an instant. 'We mun do summut for 'em,' said he to Wilson.

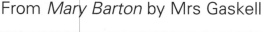

From *Mary Barton* by Mrs Gaskell

Name _____   Date _____

Poor housing – 2

Report of the state of the inhabitants and their dwellings in Church Lane, St Giles's in 'Journal of the Statistical Society of London' (1848)

House No 2
Ground Floor – 2 rooms
Number of families 3; consisting of 22 souls. Number of persons ill, 2, fever and measles. State of rooms filthy; state of furniture, bad and dirty…No. of bedsteads 6 in the two rooms. A man and his wife and children occupying a bed for a week, pay 3 shillings. The yard of this house, 6ft square, in a very bad state. The privy has no seat or door; night-soil scattered about the yard. Liquid filth under the broken pavement.

The Cellar
3 beds, dirty, 11 persons

First Floor
1 room – 16 occupants, 3 beds

Second Floor
1 room – 12 occupants, 3 beds – Three females sleep in one bed. A son aged 22 sleeps with his mother.

How many people live in this house of five rooms?

_____

How many people live in your house and how many rooms do you have?

_____

What would it be like to live in this Victorian house?

_____

Why did people put up with these conditions do you think?

_____

THE VICTORIANS: Victorian towns and town life
How did people get about in Victorian towns? Page 29
PHOTOCOPIABLE

Name _____   Date _____

Advances in transport quiz

Match up the right dates with the invention of new transport systems.

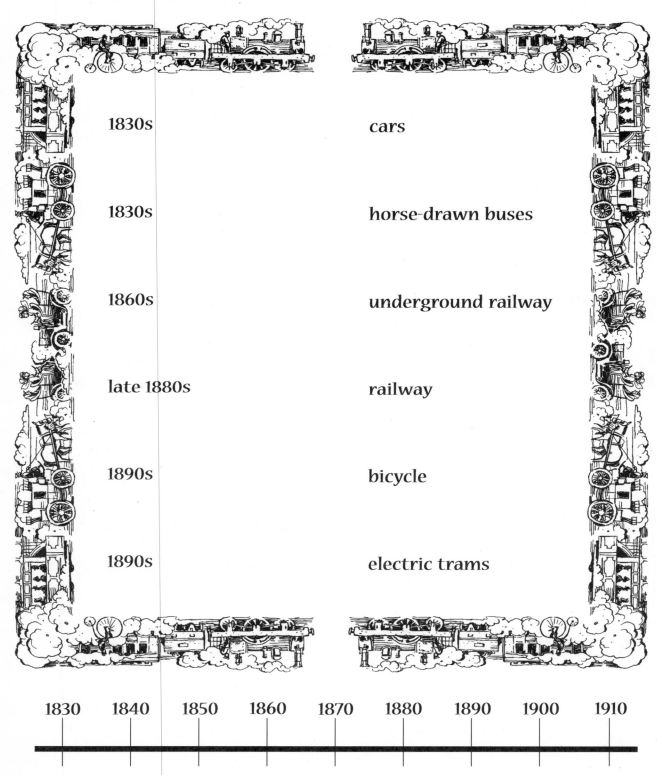

1830s   cars

1830s   horse-drawn buses

1860s   underground railway

late 1880s   railway

1890s   bicycle

1890s   electric trams

1830   1840   1850   1860   1870   1880   1890   1900   1910

Life in the workhouse

[The board] contracted to supply periodically small quantities of oatmeal: and issued 3 meals of thin gruel a day, with an onion twice a week and half a roll on Sundays…The room in which the boys were fed, was a large stone hall, with a copper at one end: out of which the master…ladled the gruel at meal-times…The bowls never wanted washing. Oliver Twist and his companions suffered the tortures of slow starvation for three months…lots were cast for who should walk up to the master at supper that evening and ask for more, and it fell to Oliver Twist.

From *The Adventures of Oliver Twist* by Charles Dickens

Greenwood pretended to be a pauper to get a night's accommodation in the workhouse to see what it was really like for the poor. In the dormitory he heard a tale. A man was talking about when he was young and staying in the workhouse at Stepney. This boy was allowed out to visit his mother as a treat. A woman living nearby asked the boy to call in at the Deaf and Dumb school on his way back to the workhouse and take a message to her daughter there. The little girl was attracted by the boy's jacket buttons. 'Presently she takes a fancy for some of my jacket buttons – brass uns they was, with the name of the 'house' on 'em – and I cuts four on 'em off and gives her. Well, when I give her them blow me if she didn't want one of the brass buckles off my shoes. Well, you mightn't think it, but I gave her that too.'
'Didn't yer get into a row when you got back?' some listener asked.
'Rather! Got kep without dinner and walloped as well, as I wouldn't tell what I'd done with 'em. Then they was goin' to wallop me again, so I thought I'd cheek it out: so I up and told the master all about it.'
'And got it wuss?'[worse]
'No I didn't. The master give me new buttons and a buckle without saying another word.'

James Greenwood, 'A Night in the Workhouse' appeared in Pall Mall Gazette 1866

PHOTOCOPIABLE
THE VICTORIANS: Victorian towns and town life
What help was given to the poor in towns? Page 31

Workhouse rules of conduct

Any pauper who shall neglect to observe such of the regulations shall be punished by confinement to a separate room, with or without an alteration of the diet...[bread and water diet]

[A pauper shall not]

make a noise when silence is ordered to be kept;

use obscene or profane language;

refuse or neglect to work;

play at cards or other games of chance;

be deemed disorderly;

repeat any offence or commit more than one offence with in seven days.

THE VICTORIANS: Victorian towns and town life
How did the Victorians deal with crime? Page 33
PHOTOCOPIABLE

Crime and penalties

Here are some extracts from writings about child criminals and the penalties they faced. Read them and consider their effectiveness in stopping crime.

Matthew Davenport Hill Q.C. giving evidence to the Select Committee on Criminal and Destitute Juveniles
'Are there any classes of children…peculiarly liable to crime?'
   'Yes. The first class is the children of criminals: they are hereditary criminals: they are trained to crime. Then illegitimate children: …illegitimate children form a very large class of juvenile criminals. Orphans for obvious reasons, form another class…and no doubt the children of the very poor form a class. But…poverty, though a cause of crime, is a very much smaller cause than is usually supposed.'

Extract from the Journal of the Chaplain of the County House of Correction, Preston, Lancashire.

March 13 1852 – The only juvenile committed during the week is that of a child aged ten, named John Marshall, but it is his fourth committal: his offence being 'sleeping out'…This poor child is the younger brother of William M. aged 11 who was discharged on the 20th, from an 18 months imprisonment for robbing a shop-till, in conjunction with another boy of 14, whom it was necessary to sentence to transportation. The prison history of the two brothers is:

William Marshall aged 11 (born 1841)
Committed June 1849 sentenced 1 month (aged 8)
   "   Nov 1849 sentenced 6 months (aged 8)
   "   Aug 1850 sentenced 18 months (aged 9)

John Marshall aged 10 (born 1842)
Committed June 1849 – sentenced 1 month (aged 7)
   "   June 1850 – for attempt at felony (theft) 14 days (aged 8)
   "   Dec 1850 – for another attempt at felony 14 days (aged 8)
   "   Mar 1852 – for sleeping out 7 days (aged 10)

The chaplain recounts the family circumstances of the boys, a drunken father who battered his first wife to death and attempted to drown the boys. There was no money for food and it was unsafe for the boys to be in the home.

THE VICTORIANS: Victorian towns and town life

How did the Victorians deal with crime? Page 33

Name _____   Date _____

Friday, March 15th 1845

Town Recorder

Name _____   Date _____

World War II worksheet

Answer these questions in full sentences.

When was World War II started?

_____

Why did the war begin?

_____

Who was fighting whom?

_____

Why were children evacuated from cities into the countryside in 1939?

_____

What happened at Dunkirk in 1940?

_____

What was the Battle of Britain and who won?

_____

Who was Winston Churchill and why was he famous?

_____

What did the people of Britain have to endure during the war?

_____

What was the name of the Allied offensive that began the fight back against Germany?

_____

When did the war end and who won?

_____

Name _____   Date _____

Timeline

Record on the timeline the following events:

Germany invades Poland
Britain declares war on Germany
The Dunkirk evacuation
The Battle of Britain
The Blitz begins
D-Day landings
VE Day
VJ Day

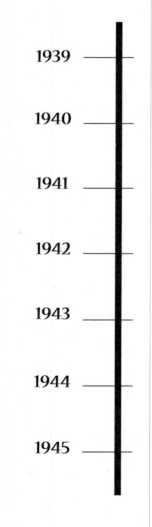

1939 ——

1940 ——

1941 ——

1942 ——

1943 ——

1944 ——

1945 ——

BRITAIN SINCE 1930: **What was life like in Britain during World War II?**
What was it like to be evacuated? Page 39

PHOTOCOPIABLE

Evacuation quotes

These extracts are from people remembering what it was like to be evacuated during the war. Read them and decide what were the good things and bad things about evacuation.

'...with about forty little children. I had to queue up to have a label tied to my braces and I had to carry my gas-mask over my shoulder...The buses took us to Lime St Station where we got on a train to Nantwich...For me, the evacuation seemed like a great adventure.' **Matt**

Leaving
'I was frightened to death. I had never been away from home before...Now I had the job of looking after three younger sisters...I was only thirteen at the time.' **Betty**

Arriving
'When we arrived in Stanton we were taken to the village hall. I felt like a refugee. I was deeply upset and worried about my sister. People kept coming in and out of the hall to choose children – it was just like a market! I was determined not to let anyone split up our family...however we were split up.' **Betty**

Betty remembered that even before she and her sister were allowed into the house, they were taken into a shed in the back garden where their foster mother poured paraffin and vinegar onto their hair, and then subjected them to intensive combing, until she was convinced that they were both scrupulously clean. They were then allowed inside the bathroom where they were each given a hot bath and their hair was washed.

Life as an evacuee
'Our bedroom was very nice but we were given jugs of hot water and bowls for our morning wash. The people were kind, they tried to make us welcome, but we never felt part of the family. We ate breakfast in the kitchen, but we ate all together in the evening.'

'I was very upset at the time, but I just had to do as I was told...I was expected to help with the housework as a re-payment for her taking us in. I never had time to play. I had too much to do in the house...I was the maid. I also had to go to school as well as looking after my younger sister.' **Betty**

'On the way home from school we often had gang fights. The Wenlock kids used to mock us...When we'd settled down we used to get involved in tough games and bad behaviour. We'd have competitions with local kids about who could throw the furthest. Then we'd get old tyres and get inside them and roll downhill.' **Jimmy**

Richard had a difficult time. He was billetted with a woman who locked them out for much of the time. 'She told us to go out and not come back until nine o'clock...As it got dark and cold we all piled into the outside lavatory...Charlie whimpered with the cold and I cuddled him like my mother...Ten o'clock came and went before we heard the bolt being drawn back...stiffly we followed her into the kitchen where we were told to get to bed quickly.'

From Joan Boyce, *Pillowslips and Gas-Masks*, 1989 Liver Press

BRITAIN SINCE 1930: **What was life like in Britain during World War II?**
What was rationing? Page 42
PHOTOCOPIABLE

Rationing

Weekly food rations for one	Free foods
Bacon and ham 4oz (100gm) Meat usually 8oz (225g) (worth 1 shilling and 2d (6p)) Butter 2oz (50g) Cheese 2oz (50g) Margarine 4oz (100g) Milk 2 pints Sugar 8oz (225g) Jam 2oz (50g) Tea 2oz (50g) Eggs 1	British grown vegetables British grown fruit

**Chart for clothes rationing
Limit 60 coupons a year**

Women	Men
Coat 14 coupons Dress 11 coupons Nightdress 8 coupons Skirt 7 coupons Briefs 2 coupons Shoes 5 coupons Stockings 2 coupons per pair	Coat 16 coupons Trousers 13 coupons Shirt 8 coupons Underpants 4 coupons Shoes 7 coupons

PHOTOCOPIABLE

Reminiscences about rationing

'I couldn't help thinking how marvellous it must have been, before the war, to go into the grocers and just ask for a couple of pounds of sugar without having to worry about ration books. We could have made all the strawberry jam we wanted then…"You can't have any more socks, there's no more coupons left!"…"No we can't have tinned fruit for tea, I've no more points!" Mother used to dry apples and store them in air-tight containers…sometimes when the meat ration had been used, we had to make do with hot soup and dumplings as the main meal.' Beryl Wade, *Storm Over the Mersey*, 1990 Countywise Ltd

An American journalist remarked 'My house has had no sugar for three days. Last evening my meal was onions and potatoes.' Marion Yaas *The Home Front* (Documentary History Series, Wayland 1971)

Queuing
According to one journalist 'most of the queues took about forty-five minutes to pass through. One queue contained 120 women lined up to get one pound of new potatoes each. In another, a woman stood for nearly three hours and came away with half a pound of tomatoes, the potatoes having gone before her turn came.' Marion Yaas *The Home Front* (Documentary History Series, Wayland 1971)

PHOTOCOPIABLE

BRITAIN SINCE 1930: **What was life like in Britain during World War II?**
Why were propaganda and censorship employed during the war? Page 43

Name _____ Date _____

Propaganda

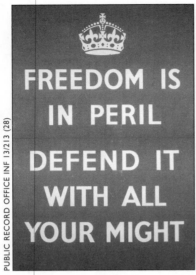

1. Look at the first poster.
What is this poster trying to make you think?

_____

War had just been declared. What would this poster make you feel about the war and your part in it?

_____

2. Look at the Keep Mum poster.
What does the poster mean by 'Keep Mum'?

_____

What is the message conveyed by this poster? (What does it want you to do?)

_____

3. Were these posters effective, do you think?_____

4. Why did the Government need to produce these posters?

PHOTOCOPIABLE

Censorship

15th JULY 1940

MR CHURCHILL AND AN INVASION

READY, UNDISMAYED, TO MEET IT WE SEEK NO TERMS AND ASK NO MERCY. LONDON IN RUINS – BETTER THAN ENSLAVEMENT

Mr Churchill, in a broadcast to British Empire and American listeners last night, reaffirmed his confidence in the determination and ability of this country to resist invasion and, when the time comes, to list the dark curse of Hitler from our age. He declared: **"Be the ordeal sharp or long, or both, we shall seek no terms, we shall tolerate no parley. We may show mercy, but we shall ask none."**

Never before had Britain had an army comparable in quality, equipment or numbers with to-day's. London itself, fought street by street, could easily devour a entire hostile army, and we would rather see London laid in ruins and ashes than that it should be abjectly enslaved.

Looking to the future, Mr Churchill declared that we must prepare not only for 1941, but for 1942, "when the war will, I trust, take a different form from the defensive in which it has hitherto been bound."

The Prime Minister said that in a week the Royal Air Force and Fighter Command had shot down more than five to one of the German aircraft which tried to attack convoys in the Channel.

Read the whole text then look at the bold, highlighted text.

1) Why has the newspaper made these sentences stand out?
2) If this was all you read of the article what impression would you get of the way the war was going?
3) Look at the final sentences. Why have these been included?
4) Does this piece reflect the true situation following the evacuation of troops from Dunkirk, do you think?
5) Identify some of the emotive words in the text. What are these words trying to make the reader feel?

PHOTOCOPIABLE

VE Day

Here are some reminiscences of the day peace was declared.

'The whole country went wild with joy. Various Royal Navy Commands in Liverpool held a special service in the Open Air at the Pier Head. Bonfires were lit all over the City. Red, white and blue flew triumphantly from every window….My father got out a large Union Jack and hung it on a big flag pole from the bedroom window. The whole of City Road was a mass of flags and bunting, as were all the side streets. Street parties were planned and I ran off to Dyson Street where arrangements for our party were already well in hand. …Father made me a red, white and blue hat from some old crepe paper…Long tables… were laid out down the centre of the street and the food carefully placed on it. Everyone lent chairs, crockery and cutlery and a huge bonfire was laid ready: this would be set alight later in the evening. We made a huge effigy of Hitler and this was put on top of the bonfire.' *Storm Over the Mersey*, Beryl Wade,1990 Countywise Ltd

'My Aunty Al got her piano out and played in the street and everyone was dancing and singing. The party went on all through the night.' *The Home Front* (Witness History Series) Stewart Ross, Wayland, 1990

A journalist wrote 'In one crowded, crazy day, in one small patch of London, I've been passionately kissed by three girls…I've sung Land of Hope and Glory till I'm hoarse…I've climbed my first and positively my last lamp post, and I've nearly persuaded myself, but not quite, that the war is over…Peace is something you need time to get used to.' *The Home Front*, (The Documentary History Series), Marion Yaas, Wayland, 1987

'I thought of those who had been dear to us who had not lived to see this…and then went indoors to stand looking at the sleeping faces of my two little sons, whose lives lay before then in a world of peace.' *We'll Meet Again*, by Vera Lynn with Robin Cross and Jenny de Gex

PHOTOCOPIABLE

Name _____   Date _____

The war is over!

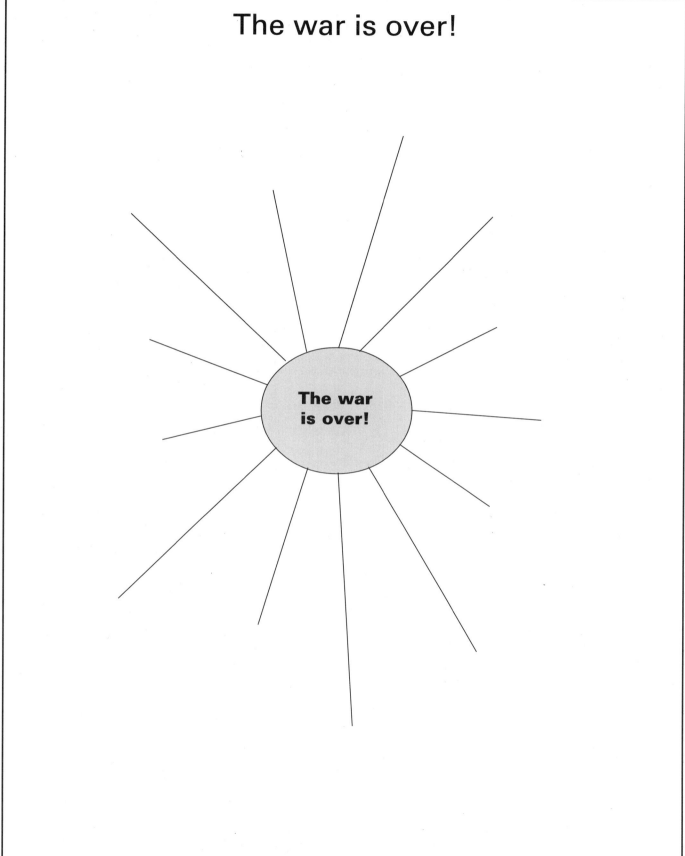

Events and changes 1930–2000

National/International events	Technological change	Social change
1930s Great Depression	**1947** Mass-production of penicillin	**1930s** Cinema and radio very popular
1939-45 World War II	**1956** Polio vaccine made available to children	**1936** BBC begins broadcasting on TV
1944 Education Act		
1948 National Heath Service comes into being	**1957** Sputnik launched. First space satellite	**1939–52** Rationing of food and clothing
1953 Coronation of Elizabeth II	**1967** Colour TV available	**1955** Rock and roll music comes over from America
1950–3 Korean War	**1969** First man lands on moon	
1956 Martin Luther King leads Civil Rights Movement in America	**1969** Concorde supersonic plane comes into service	**1940s–1960s** Commonwealth citizens invited to work in Britain
	1971 Silicon microchip invented	**1960s** Music revolution (Beatles, Rolling Stones)
1968 Beginning of Troubles in Northern Ireland	**1978** First test-tube baby born	**1960s** Youth culture emerges
1973 UK enters the EEC	**1980** First fax sent	**1960s** Flower Power and Peace Movement
1975 Referendum for remaining in European Common Market. Result is yes	**1990s** Mobile phones become commonplace	**1967** Colour TV
	1999 Dolly the sheep cloned	**1970s** Unions engage strike action (winter of discontent)
1975 Sex Discrimination Act		
1976 Race Relations Act		**1979–90s** The Thatcher years
1982 Falklands War		**1981** Race riots in Brixton, Bristol and Liverpool
1985 Equal Opportunities Act		
1990–1 The Gulf War		**1988** National Curriculum to be taught in all state schools
1997 BSE crisis		**1997** BSE crisis
1999 Serbian offensive		**2000** Millennium celebrations
2000 Millennium celebrations		

1930   1940   1950   1960   1970   1980   1990   2000

Name _____   Date _____

Looking at change 1930–2000

What have been some of the key changes between 1930 and now?

_____

_____

_____

What do you consider the most important change to affect people during this period?

_____

_____

Why do you think this is the most important change?

_____

_____

_____

_____

_____

_____

_____

_____

PHOTOCOPIABLE

Name _____   Date _____

Britain since1930 game

Flower Power

World War II

Rock and roll comes to Britain   1930 ——|—

Race Relations Act

                                                      1940 ——|—
Coronation of Queen Elizabeth II

BSE crisis   1950 ——|—

First test-tube baby

                                                      1960 ——|—
First nuclear bomb dropped

Troubles begin in Northern Ireland   1970 ——|—

Gulf War

Falklands War   1980 ——|—

Men land on moon

                                                      1990 ——|—
Apollo 13 mission aborted

Beatles record their hits   2000 ——|—

Silicon chip invented

Mobile phones commonly used

Millennium celebrations

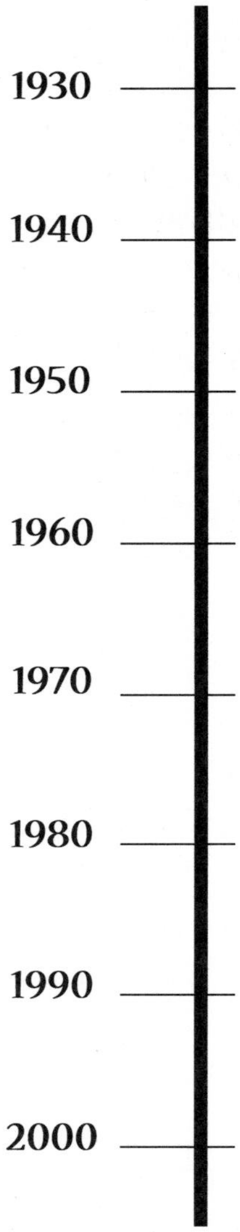

Name _____   Date _____

Getting started on your research project – 1

Our aspect is: _____

Our researchers are: _____

Key questions

Think about your topic. What do you need to find out about? Try to come up with some big questions that will help you to order your research. For example, if your topic was life at work you might have these key questions:
a) What were conditions like for workers in the 1930s, the 1960s and now?
b) What sort of jobs were available in this town in the 1930s, 1960s and now?
c) What laws were made during these decades that altered the way people worked?
d) Were there any inventions or big national events that affected life at work?
List your key questions now. You may add to these or change them during your research.

_____

_____

_____

_____

_____

_____

_____

_____

_____

_____

? ? ? ? ? ? ? ? ? ? ? ? ? ? ? ? ? ? ? ?

Getting started on your research project – 2

Plan of action

1. Work out what each one of you will do. You may decide to work independently on different books or sources, or together. Time is short. Be efficient.

2. Take a question and try to find some answers.

3. Use information books and CD-ROMs first. Use index, contents lists and subheadings to get you to the important and relevant information quickly.

4. Make notes summarising what the book says. You can write in short form for example with points. Do not copy word for word. It will take too long. Make sure you also record the book's author and title and the page you got the information from. Also note if it has good pictures you might use later.

5. Download and print out important information from CD-ROMs or Internet sites if practical. Otherwise make notes at the terminal and record the website address or CD-ROM page.

6. Keep all information gathered in one file.

7. Meet with your partner often to talk through and share information and re-organise work.

8. Get help from the teacher if you do not understand what you are reading or you are having problems.

Remember you are responsible for your own historical enquiry and the display. Do the best work that you can.

BRITAIN SINCE 1930: **How has life changed since 1930?**
What can our families tell us about the past? Page 50

PHOTOCOPIABLE

Name _____   Date _____

Eye-witness questionnaire

Date _____

We are finding out about _____ as part of our history project on Life since 1930. We would be very grateful if you could answer the following questions.

What is your name? _____

When were you born? _____

Specific topic questions

_____

_____

_____

_____

_____

_____

_____

_____

_____

_____

_____

_____

Thank-you

Name _____   Date _____

Presenting your research

By now you will have lots of information. Think about what you must have on your display and plan the layout together in the space below, taking into consideration the shape and space you have available.

Our display plan

Presenting information
Are you going to use:
• written or typed reports?
• pictures (if so, what medium, e.g. paints, felt-tipped pens)?
• collage or models?
• computer graphics or illustrations?
• electronic entry on data file or web page?

Organise your information into appropriate groups. Read it through and then begin to work on one piece. Do your writing or word-processing first. Do a rough draft then edit it together as a pair. Then copy it up. Next do pictures and computer-based work. Finally do model-making.

   Lay out the display approximately using Blu-tack or similar. When you are both satisfied with the layout, secure it firmly, or let the teacher know it needs stapling. Don't forget to add a title and a name label to your display. You've earned that recognition.

Name _____ Date _____

What do we know about the Ancient Greeks and what do we want to know about them?

What do we know about the Ancient Greeks?	What do we want to know about them?	How will I find out?

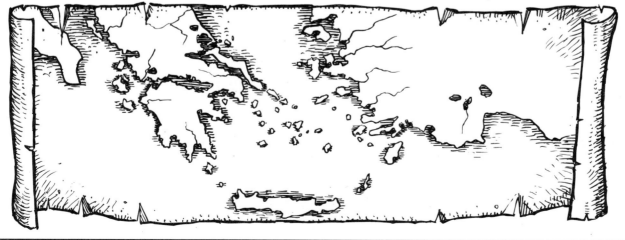

PHOTOCOPIABLE

ANCIENT GREECE: Who were the Ancient Greeks?
What did people look like in Ancient Greece? Page 57

Name _____   Date _____

How good is the evidence?

We get a lot of evidence about daily life in Ancient Greece from pictures on Greek vases. How good is this evidence?

Source of material	Primary or secondary source	What does the vase tell you about life in Ancient Greece?	What does the vase not tell you?
Greek vase in a museum in the UK			
Greek vase in a museum in Greece			
Photograph of a vase			
Replica of the vase in the classroom			
Illustration of a vase			
Vase on a computer screen from the British Museum collection			

Name _____   Date _____

Asking questions

Topic chosen: _____

Books used: _____

Other sources (e.g. websites, CD-ROM) _____

_____

Three major pieces of information I have discovered about my topic:

1. _____

_____

2. _____

_____

3. _____

_____

Quiz question for the class:

Name _____   Date _____

Asking questions about everyday life in Ancient Greece

Choose one of these topics and find two other questions to ask about it. Make sure you do not know the answers.

When?   Who?

Homes	**Education**
1. What furniture did the Ancient Greeks have?	1. Who went to school in Ancient Greece?
2.	2.
3.	3.
Transport	**Slaves**
1. What were Greek ships like?	1. Who were slaves in Ancient Greece?
2.	2.
3.	3.
Sports	**Food**
1. What sports did people play and watch?	1. What food can I find in pictures about Ancient Greece?
2.	2.
3.	3.

Now find the answers to your questions.

ANCIENT GREECE: **Who were the Ancient Greeks?**
Who were some famous Ancient Greeks? Page 61

PHOTOCOPIABLE

Fact or fiction?

Name of person	Famous for	Fact (did they really exist?)	Fiction (is this person a myth?)
Herakles			
Alexander the Great			
Helen of Troy			
Aristotle			
Philip of Macedonia			
Herodotos			
Zeus			
Pericles			
Homer			
Nike			

What is your evidence that _____ really lived?

PHOTOCOPIABLE

ANCIENT GREECE: Who were the Ancient Greeks?
Who were some famous Ancient Greeks. Page 61

Name _____   Date _____

Alexander the Great

Who was Alexander the Great?

_____

Who influenced him as a child?

_____

What effect did this have on him?

_____

What was his greatest wish?

_____

How did he make his wish come true?

_____

_____

Alexander the Great was the son of the Macedonian king Philip II. He was one of the greatest military leaders of all time. As a child, Alexander was influenced by his teacher, the Greek philosopher Aristotle. Aristotle taught Alexander to love philosophy and Greek ways. Alexander's greatest wish was to spread the Greek legacy. To turn his wish into reality, Alexander conquered lands, built cities modelled on Greek cities and encouraged a blend of cultures and ideas.

Name _____   Date _____

Athens

Athens and Sparta

Sparta

These statements refer to either Athens or Sparta. Write them in the correct column.

a strong army

ate plain food

built an Acropolis   a strong navy

girls given greater freedom

had harsh laws   gained wealth by conquering peoples around them   a military state

many beautiful buildings

Athens	Sparta

Can you find any other differences between the two city states?

PHOTOCOPIABLE

Reviewing vocabulary

tragedy

peninsula

legacy

assembly

Acropolis

polis

philosophy

myth

democracy

monarchy

Match the word with the statement.

● The Ancient Greeks did not like this form of government because the power was in the hands of the king or queen.

● This is made up of a city, and all the land surrounding it. This type of political organisation was typical of Ancient Greece.

● Sometimes this is called the birthplace of Western civilisation, this hill was the centre of ancient Athens.

● These are plays which usually end sadly.

● This is what one generation hands down to another.

● The House of Commons and the Welsh and Scottish Parliaments are examples of this law-making body, which is basic to all world democracies.

● The relationship between the gods and human beings is one of the things explained in this type of story.

● This search for truth is concerned with basic questions about life and our place in it.

● The Ancient Greeks were the first to practise this form of government.

● This term describes land that is surrounded by water on three sides.

Name _____   Date _____

The Parthenon

You have been asked to re-create the Parthenon. Use non-fiction texts to find out what it might have looked like. Draw your extensions on this illustration. When you have finished, decide how the new Parthenon could be used.

PHOTOCOPIABLE

ANCIENT GREECE: Why is the history of Ancient Greece important to us?
How have Greek ideas influenced our buildings? Page 67

Greek columns

Greek architects invented three 'orders' of architecture. These were called the Doric, Ionic and Corinthian. The names refer to different kinds of columns and decorations.

Doric

Ionic

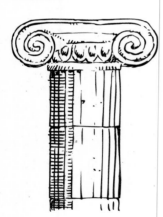
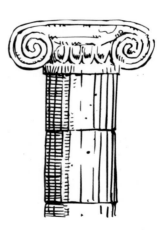
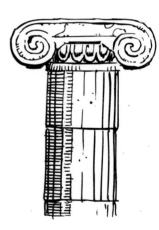

Corinthian

ANCIENT GREECE: Why is the history of Ancient Greece important to us?

How has our language been influenced by the Ancient Greeks? Page 70

Name _____   Date _____

The Greek alphabet

My name in Greek letters:

_____

Aα a	Bβ b	Γγ g	Δδ d
alpha	beta	gamma	delta
Eε e	Zζ z	Hη e	Θθ th
epsilon (short)	zeta	eta (long)	theta
Iι i	Kκ k	Λλ l	Mμ m
iota	kappa	lambda	mu
Nν n	Ξξ x	Oο o	Ππ p
nu	xi	omicron (short)	pi
Pρ r	Σσ s	Tτ t	Yυ u
rho	sigma	tau	upsilon
Φφ ph	Xχ kh	Ψψ ps	Ωω o
phi	chi	psi	omega (long)

PHOTOCOPIABLE

ANCIENT GREECE: Why is the history of Ancient Greece important to us?
How have Greek ideas influenced our understanding of citizenship? Page 71

Democracy in Ancient Athens

Use non-fiction texts to investigate being a citizen in Athens. Use them to answer these questions

1. What do you think these men are doing?

2. Who could be a citizen in Athens?

3. What age were they when they became citizens?

4. Could women citizens vote?

5. Who could not be a citizen?

6. What happened to someone if they did not vote?

7. What other groups might these men be members of?

8. What happened if Athenian citizens wrote the name of the same man on a piece of pottery called an ostraka?

Democracy in the UK
Who can vote in the UK today?

Who cannot vote?

What happens to citizens if they do not vote?

Name _____ Date _____

Cortes' expedition to the Aztec Empire

PHOTOCOPIABLE

THE AZTECS: **When and where was the Aztec Empire?**
Who were the Aztecs? Page 76

Name _____ Date _____

Blank timeline

Key dates

1250 (approximately): Aztecs reach the valley of Mexico.

1325–1345: the tribe that came to be known as the Aztecs settle on land in the valley of Mexico, and build the village which became Tenochtitlan.

1426: the Aztecs join forces with neighbouring people against the dominant tribe of the Tepanecs.

1428: the Aztecs overthrow the Tepanecs.

1440–1468: Montezuma I expands the Aztec Empire through conquest.

1450–1454: famine.

1492: Columbus lands in the West Indies.

1502: Montezuma becomes Emperor.

1517: the Spanish expedition to Yucatan returns to Cuba where Cortes is chief magistrate, bringing gold stolen from the temples.

1519 (February): Cortes lands in Mexico.

1519 (April): Cortes sails to Vera Cruz (settlement on east coast of Mexico), meets Aztec visitors who bring gifts including gold, and makes allies of the local people.

1519 (August): Cortes destroys his ships at Vera Cruz because some of his men want to return to Cuba.

1519 (November): Cortes enters Tenochtitlan and is welcomed by Montezuma. After a few days, Montezuma is taken captive by the Spanish. Cortes leaves Tenochtitlan to fight an expeditionary force. Aztecs rise against the Spanish left in Tenochtitlan. Cortes returns to the city.

1520: Montezuma II is killed by one of his subjects.

1520 (July): the Spanish army fights its way out of Tenochtitlan.

1520–May 1521: Cortes regroups his forces, and makes alliances with local tribes.

1521 (April): Cortes lays siege to Tenochtitlan.

1521 (August): Tenochtitlan falls to the Spanish and is destroyed, and the Aztec king Cuahtenoc is killed.

1547: Cortes dies in Spain.

PHOTOCOPIABLE

Aztec society

Cut the pictures out and put them in order from the most important person to the least important.

 Judge	 Merchant	 Farmer
 Slave	 Emperor	 Priest
 Noble	 Advisor to the Emperor	 Soldier
 Craftworker	 Knight	 Child

THE AZTECS: When and where was the Aztec Empire?

How was the Aztec civilisation organised? Page 77

Name _____   Date _____

Researching Aztec life

Your Aztec role is: _____

Use the resources to find information about your life. Make notes.

Home	Clothes
Food	Work
Leisure	Other

PHOTOCOPIABLE

THE AZTECS: **When and where was the Aztec Empire?**
Who was Cortes and why did he lead an expedition into Aztec territory? Page 78

Cortes

PHOTOCOPIABLE

Looking for clues about Cortes

1. What Hernan wanted was not the dreary routine of a lawyer, but a life of adventure. His thoughts turned to the New World. Soon he was packing his bags and heading south for Seville, a bustling port where caravels were coming in weekly for the Indies… In 1504, when he was 19, he finally reached Hispaniola [Haiti], and was granted land and Indian slaves to work it… Seven years later, Cortes joined a force sent to conquer Cuba and settled in the new colony.

Discovery magazine, 1991

2. In 1519 a Spaniard called Hernan Cortes sailed from Cuba to Yucatan (now part of Mexico). He waved a special flag as he went on board his ship. The words were in Latin and… meant "Friends, let us follow the cross, and if we have faith we will surely conquer in this sign".

Triggs, T.D. *Primary History Explorations and Encounters* 1992

PHOTOCOPIABLE

THE AZTECS: **When and where was the Aztec Empire?**
Who was Cortes and why did he lead an expedition into Aztec territory? Page 78

Name _____ Date _____

Why did Cortes go to Mexico? (Writing frame)

I want to explain why Cortes went to Mexico.
There were several reasons for this.
The main reason was

_____

_____

Another reason was

_____

_____

Another reason was

_____

_____

The final reason was

_____

_____

So now you can understand why Cortes went to Mexico.

Name _____   Date _____

Why did Cortes go to Mexico? (Writing frame)

Cortes went to Mexico for several reasons.
The most important reason is

_____

The evidence for this is

_____

Another reason is

_____

The evidence for this is

_____

Another reason is

_____

The evidence for this is

_____

The final reason is

_____

The evidence for this is

_____

THE AZTECS: When and where was the Aztec Empire?
PHOTOCOPIABLE   How and why did Cortes defeat the Aztecs? Page 80

What do the sources tell us about the meeting between Cortes and Montezuma?

1.

When Cortes saw, heard, and was told that the great Montezuma was approaching, he dismounted from his horse, and when he came near to Montezuma each bowed deeply to the other. Montezuma welcomed our captain, and Cortes speaking through Dona Marina, answered by wishing him very good health. Cortes, I think offered Montezuma his right hand, but Montezuma refused it and extended his own. Then Cortes brought out a necklace which he had been holding. It was made of those elaborately worked and coloured glass beads called margaritas, of which I have spoken, and was strung on a gold cord and dipped in musk to give it a good odour. This he hung round the great Montezuma's neck, and as he did he attempted to embrace him. But the great princes who stood round Montezuma grasped Cortes' arm to prevent him, for they considered it an indignity.

2.

Thus Motecuhzoma went out to meet them, there in Huitzillan. He presented many gifts to the captain and his commanders, those who had come to make war. He showered gifts upon them and hung flowers around their necks; he gave them necklaces of flowers and bands of flowers to adorn them; he set garlands of flowers upon their heads. Then he hung the gold necklaces around their necks and gave them presents of every sort as gifts of welcome.

When Motecuhzoma had given necklaces to each one, Cortes asked him: "Are you Motecuhzoma? Are you the king? Is it true that you are the king Motecuhzoma?"

And the king said: "Yes, I am Motecuhzoma." Then he stood up to address Cortes; he came forward, bowed his head low and addressed him in these words: "Our Lord, you are weary. The journey has tired you, but now you have arrived on the earth. You have come to your city, Mexico. You have come here to sit on your throne, to sit under its canopy".

3.

Moctezuma himself came out to meet us with some two hundred nobles, all barefoot and dressed in some kind of uniform also very rich, in fat more than the others. They came forward in two long lines keeping close to the walls of the street, which is very broad and fine and so straight that one can see from one end of the other, though it is two thirds of a league (two miles) in length and lined on both sides with very beautiful large houses, both private dwellings and temples. Moctezuma himself was borne along in the middle of the street with two lords, one on his right hand and one of his left… All three were dressed in similar fashion except that Moctezuma wore shoes whereas the others were barefoot… As he drew near I dismounted and advanced alone to embrace, but the two lords prevented me from touching him…they…kissing the earth…While speaking to Moctezuma I took off a necklace of pearls and crystals which I was wearing and threw it round his neck.

4

The marques and his men followed another causeway that crossed the lake, all the way to Mexico, and Montezuma came out to meet him, after first having sent a nephew with many men and provisions. Montezuma came down the centre of the street, and all the rest of the people along the sides of the walls, according to the custom. He had the marques lodged near the chamber of the idols, in a courtyard whose halls were more than large enough to take care of all the marques' men and many of the Tlaxcalan and Cholulan Indians who had come with the Spaniards to serve them.

| 1 Diaz (one of Cortes' officers) | 3 Cortes |
| 2 Aztec – Broken Spears | 4 Tapia (soldier with Cortes) |

PHOTOCOPIABLE

Why were the Aztecs defeated?
Comparing armies

PHOTOCOPIABLE

THE AZTECS: When and where was the Aztec Empire?
How and why did Cortes defeat the Aztecs? Page 80

Why were the Aztecs defeated?

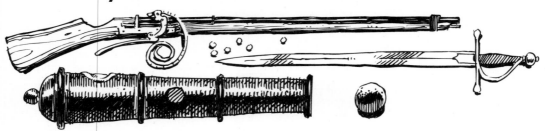

Other tribes in Mexico helped the Spanish soldiers.	The Spaniards had guns, cannons and gunpowder.
Aztec warriors wore armour made of stiff cloth. Spanish soldiers wore metal armour.	Many Aztecs caught smallpox from the Spanish soldiers.
Aztec warriors wanted to take prisoners and did not kill their enemies in battle.	Cortes was a strong leader.
Spanish soldiers were trained to work together.	The Aztecs had seen omens and believed terrible things would happen.
The Spanish soldiers had wheeled transport.	The Aztecs did not have horses.
The Aztecs believed Cortes and his soldiers were gods.	The Spaniards believed that God was on their side and they were fighting to spread the Christian faith.

THE AZTECS: When and where was the Aztec Empire?
What happened to the Aztec Empire? Page 82

PHOTOCOPIABLE

What happened to the Aztec Empire?

One of the men called Navarez had smallpox; it was said that this disease entered the country, for it spread with unbelievable speed, killing thousands of Aztecs; not knowing what it was, they threw themselves into cold water to deal with the fever and this caused their death.
Diaz

PHOTOCOPIABLE

THE AZTECS: When and where was the Aztec Empire?
What happened to the Aztec Empire? Page 82

Name _____ Date _____

Different points of view

The issue we are discussing is whether the Spanish conquest of Mexico was a good thing.

Arguments for the Spanish point of view	Arguments for the Aztec point of view

My conclusion is

Name _____ Date _____

Learning about the Aztecs: primary sources

Type of source: _____
What areas of Aztec life does it tell us about?

Problems

Type of source: _____
What areas of Aztec life does it tell us about?

Problems

Type of source: _____
What areas of Aztec life does it tell us about?

Problems

Type of source: _____
What areas of Aztec life does it tell us about?

Problems

PHOTOCOPIABLE

THE AZTECS: What sources are available for the Aztecs?
How do we know about the Aztecs? Page 86

Name _____ Date _____

Aztec fact file

Aztec facts

Aspect of daily life _____

Fact _____

_____

_____

_____

_____

Source of information

Aztec facts

Aspect of daily life _____

Fact _____

_____

_____

_____

Source of information

Name _____   Date _____

Investigating Aztec artefacts

Artefact number [ ]

I think this is _____

_____

Reason _____

_____

Aspect of life _____

Artefact number [ ]

I think this is _____

_____

Reason _____

_____

Aspect of life _____

Artefact number [ ]

I think this is _____

_____

Reason _____

_____

Aspect of life _____

Why have so few artefacts survived? Give three ideas.

_____

_____

_____

_____

PHOTOCOPIABLE

THE AZTECS: **What sources are available for the Aztecs ?**
What visual sources are available for Aztec times and how reliable are they? Page 88

Name _____ Date _____

Visual sources

Type of source	Produced by	Purpose	Audience	Primary or secondary

Visual sources

Tzapotilan – the Conquest of Mexico by Cortez,
15th century Mexican artist (unknown)

© AKG LONDON

Cortez's victory over the Indians from Tabasco,
18th century Spanish artist (unknown)

© AKG LONDON

Written sources – Whose point of view? – 1

1.

When they were given the presents, the Spaniards burst into smiles; their eyes shone with pleasure; they were delighted by them. They picked up the gold and fingered it like monkeys; they seemed to be transported by joy, as if their hearts were illumined and made new. The truth is that they longed and lusted for gold. Their bodies swelled with greed, and their hunger was ravenous; they hungered like pigs for that gold. They snatched at the gold ensigns, waved them from side to side and examined every inch of them…

2.

The streets are wide and beautiful. Two or three of the main ones are built on an island but the rest are half water and half banks of soil. The people walk on the soil or ride canoes on the water. The canoes are dug out of tree trunks, and some are large enough to hold five people easily. There are other streets which are all water, so people have to go by canoe. Without their canoes they would not be able to get to their houses.
The houses belonging to the lords were so large and had so many rooms that they were amazing to see.

Written sources – Whose point of view? – 2

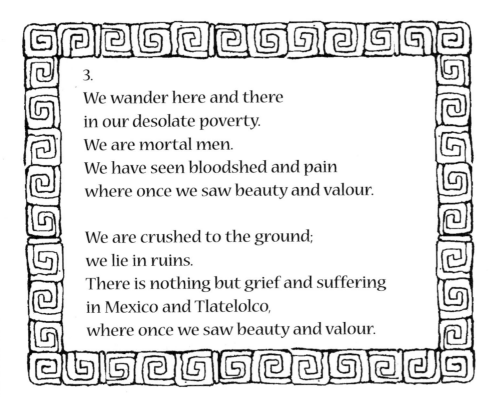

3.

We wander here and there
in our desolate poverty.
We are mortal men.
We have seen bloodshed and pain
where once we saw beauty and valour.

We are crushed to the ground;
we lie in ruins.
There is nothing but grief and suffering
in Mexico and Tlatelolco,
where once we saw beauty and valour.

4.

Their bodies are completely covered so only their faces can be seen.
Their skin is white as if it were made of lime. They have yellow hair,
though some have black. Their beards are long and yellow. They dress
in iron and wear iron casks on their heads. The deer carry them on
their backs wherever they wish to go. These deer are as tall as the roof
of a house.

PHOTOCOPIABLE

THE AZTECS: What sources are available for the Aztecs?
What written sources are available for the Aztecs? Page 90

Name _____   Date _____

Whose point of view?

Number	What does it describe?	Point of view	Reason